YOUR FUTURE IN JOBS ABROAD

ARCO-ROSEN
CAREER GUIDANCE SERIES

YOUR FUTURE IN
JOBS
ABROAD

Elmer L. Winter

arco
New York

Revised Edition
Second Arco Printing, 1976

Published by Arco Publishing Company, Inc.
219 Park Avenue South, New York, N.Y. 10003
by arrangement with Richards Rosen Press, Inc.

Library of Congress Catalog Card Number 72-114115
ISBN 0-668-02251-5

Printed in the United States of America

Contents

About the Author

IN 1948 ELMER L. WINTER had a law partner, Aaron Scheinfeld, a secretary, and an idea. In 1967 he found himself with 190,000 secretaries, 110,000 industrial workers, and a company that grossed $142,000,000 for the year.

As president and cofounder of Manpower Inc., he heads the world's largest temporary-help and complete business service, with 536 offices in 34 countries on six continents.

Elmer L. Winter is married and the father of three attractive daughters. His residence, located in the Milwaukee suburb of Fox Point near the shore of Lake Michigan, is a 75-year-old structure that offers the charm of the past with the comfort and convenience of the present. A ski enthusiast, the author relishes Wisconsin's "Winter Wonderland" in spite of the sub-zero temperatures.

Winter encourages creative efforts in others—sets the example. He designed and completed a sweeping mosaic along a high wall lining the edge of the back yard at his home, and he inspired a giant mosaic sculpture that is on the back of Manpower's headquarters on the bank of the Milwaukee River. The project is the beginning of Manpower's International Marina, a civic betterment idea to replace river blight with beauty. Winter recently sponsored the "Executives' Easel Art Show," a collection of paintings by some of the country's outstanding corporation presidents and professional leaders. The show was presented to the public in museums and galleries throughout the United States, Canada, and four European countries.

A current project in which he takes much pride is his "Operation Free Enterprise System," through which Manpower offices "adopt" foreign universities and supply them with business magazines, books, and films to open up new lines of communication in underdeveloped countries and to provide accurate information explaining American philosophy, government, history, and culture. Winter's Youthpower idea has earned a citation from the U.S. Government for the valuable service it provides. Youthpower is a nonprofit service affiliate of Manpower that has made over 20,000 summer job placements since it was founded four years ago. It is expanding to 19 other cities across the United States and Canada.

Winter is currently trying to solve some of the major problems facing business today through Manpower Research Council. He has formed a research group of over 500 personnel and industrial relations executives from this country's biggest companies, who contribute their ideas to council surveys on significant issues. Results are printed and distributed to firms throughout the country.

Winter was one of the cofounders of the Milwaukee Voluntary Equal Employment Opportunity Council, and he has been a guiding force in the development of an urban redevelopment organization composed of civic-minded businessmen who are investing private capital in an effort to bring modern, racially integrated housing to Milwaukee's central city.

Winter travels extensively and frequently addresses major groups in this country and abroad. He has been active in setting up offices for his company in Europe, the Middle East, South America, and the Far East. Winter visits these offices frequently and has developed customer relationships with many business executives abroad.

CHAPTER I

Problems in Working Abroad

"Travel! See the world and revel in the glamor and excitement of a job abroad!"

You have only to see those words to summon up visions of yourself sunning serenely on a warm beach, buying a bouquet from a colorful flower seller or exploring Old World streets. Your apartment, straight out of the last movie you saw, is immaculately kept, and you are served elegant meals by a houseboy or maid who works eighteen hours a day for almost nothing. And best of all, you are drawing a tax-exempt paycheck that will land you back on American shores with a bulging bank account.

But wait! Before you check the weight of your luggage on the bathroom scale and call the airline for a reservation, you should consider a few things.

Assuming that your approach to working abroad is a little more realistic than that pictured above, let us talk for a few minutes about some of the problems of holding a job in another country.

1. What kind of work are you capable of doing?
2. Will you work for an American firm, for a foreign business, or for the United States government?
3. At what economic level do you intend to live abroad, and would your salary meet this standard?
4. Do you speak fluently any language other than English, and are you willing to spend time and perhaps money learning another language?
5. How will you go about finding a job abroad?
6. Would you willingly be responsible for representing the best that America stands for in your role as an alien in another country?

Taking these questions one at a time, let us begin with the kind of job you might hold abroad. Contrary to popular belief, there are not openings in every field. But there *are* fields that provide varying levels of employment.

People who have found jobs on foreign soil include clerks, typists, stenographers, and general secretaries. They include doctors and nurses, teachers, social workers, economists, meteorologists, skilled tradesmen, and geologists. And, of course, scattered specialists work in other fields. Journalists, for example, can work for the government information agency or as correspondents for American publications.

Generally the same rule applies to working abroad as to working in this country: You must have a specific skill to offer an employer.

This brings us to the second point. Will you work for an American firm, for a foreign business, or for the U.S. government?

Conditions of living and working abroad vary widely depending on your employer. If you work for a foreign firm, for example, you may have to adapt yourself to very different working conditions. You may be expected, for example, to put in a twelve-hour day, six days a week. In the Middle East, you may find the "day of rest" is Friday, the Moslem sabbath, instead of Sunday.

You will certainly be expected to speak and write another language as if it were your own. You will be paid according to the local wage scale, which, when translated into dollars, may be considerably lower than your pay at home.

If you work for the U.S. government, your pay may be slightly higher, since most government jobs come under the Civil Service scale. But your responsibility as a representative of our country will also be greater. This applies to a file clerk or secretary as well as to an ambassador.

American firms operating abroad have agreed with most governments to use American employees only when and where no nationals are available. Usually this assumes a ratio of about one hundred nationals to every American employed by an American firm.

Also, it is expensive for an American business to send an employee abroad. One company president estimated that it cost nearly $50,000 to relocate one employee and his family. Granted that the cost would be lower for a single person, the fact remains that an American firm will not risk such an expenditure for someone who will not complete his contract.

Working for an American firm has many other facets that must be considered. Often the pay is notably higher in an overseas post, because specific training is required. Usually an American firm provides housing, which would be an advantage or disadvantage depending on whether you would prefer to live with other Americans.

It generally provides medical care, sometimes in its own fully staffed hospital, and educational facilities up to the high-school level. Usually teen-agers are sent either to private schools abroad or spend the high-school years with friends or relatives in America.

Living standards with an American firm are often much like those you would have in this country. You must decide for yourself what standard of living you require. Only you can know if you are willing to live in a garret for months or years just to have the experience of working abroad, or whether you would consider taking an overseas job only if servants were readily available and a swimming pool was handy.

Even if you work for an American company that conducts its business in English, which is highly unlikely, it is just about essential to learn the language of the country, either before you leave home or when you arrive on foreign soil.

To be blunt, your first task will be to "get along," and "getting along" can be difficult, if not expensive, if you speak only English. You must eat, secure lodgings, find your way around, and sometimes even locate a repairman . . . and this requires a working knowledge of the language.

Certainly, you can get a cleaning woman, repairman, and guide who speak English, but you must be prepared to pay. In another country, knowledge of English is a special skill, and people who speak it have a right to expect higher pay.

Another factor, and not an unimportant one, is that if you work for an American firm that transacts business abroad, you will be in competition for business with employees of other firms who do speak the language. Why should a German dealer buy soft drinks from a firm that does business in English if he can find one that will deal with him in German?

One young woman left her job as secretary to an executive of a large publishing firm and followed her dream of going to Paris to work. She gave up her apartment, said goodbye to her friends at a round of farewell parties and left for Paris armed with luggage, passport, shots, and enough money to "get by" until she found work. However, she soon found she did not have the most valuable asset— a knowledge of the French language.

From the beginning, she was dependent upon others, including a helpful passerby who secured a taxi for her when she left the boat train. Arriving at her hotel, after a short ride, she was unable to understand the driver when he asked for his fare, so she held out her hand with an assortment of French money. He took some and was off, and even now she has no idea whether the ride cost her 10 cents or $10.

She allotted herself a two-week "vacation" and used the time to orient herself and see the sights of Paris. Then she started her job hunt, checking the usual channels of American companies operating in Paris. Her confidence began to wane when one after another personnel director shrugged and expressed his regret that they could use only girls who could speak French. Her money was running very low and her confidence even lower when this top-notch secretary finally got a job—*four months* later.

Her job hunt might have been much easier had she learned to speak French before sailing. But we might go further and say that, almost without exception, it is wise to secure a job before leaving home.

The U.S. Chamber of Commerce states this succinctly when it asks:

"Can you risk being stranded, penniless, on foreign shores after attempts to find a job have failed?"

Coming to our last question, when you arrive as an "alien" in someone else's country you immediately become a representative of the United States. You may be the only American most of the people with whom you come into contact have ever known. The opinions you express and the way you react to what may be for you strange experiences reflect on all Americans and help to form the favorable or unfavorable view in which they are held.

What you consider light banter with a new friend may be completely misunderstood. You may find yourself spending more time explaining a joke than telling it.

If patience is not a natural trait with you, you had better learn it before going abroad. In some countries, for example, a merchant may stop to have tea, ignoring the long line of which you are part. He is sorry if you are late for your next appointment, but surely you could not have expected him to let his tea get cold.

Certainly, if you have opinions on religion or the practice of it, or on politics, you should keep them to yourself.

A person who has not traveled abroad falls easily into the idea that anyone who does not speak flawless English is in some way childish. Remember, however, he may be thinking this of you and of your attempts to speak his language.

In conclusion, jobs abroad are available for anyone who is qualified and who wants one enough to accept discomfort, hard work, and sometimes sacrifice.

If you are one of these, if you want the wonderful experience of learning to know intimately a culture other than your own, if you long to see another part of the world so much that you are willing to do almost anything to see it, if you have a skill that might help you finance part of your expanding "education," this book is for you.

I shall try to help you through the intricacies of foreign ways, work permits, pay scales, and taxes to foreign governments and at home. I shall give you suggestions on where and how such jobs may be found. I shall try to give you a picture of what it is like to live and work abroad and how to get along. I shall talk about work-study programs and the Peace Corps opportunities. I shall try to tell you where the greatest opportunities are for women and for men abroad.

And finally, having gone this far, I shall try to help you pack your suitcase.

CHAPTER II

Language

I have spoken in the first chapter of how necessary language is for "getting along" in another country, which indeed would be your first job upon arriving on foreign soil. If you were not working for an American company that provided housing, you would have to find a place to stay. This can be done without speaking another language, but it is not easy. If you have a friend where you are working, perhaps he could help you. Or you might obey an American-oriented impulse to look in the classified columns of the newspaper—provided, of course, that you were in a major city that had an English-language newspaper. Many foreign cities have agencies that will help you secure lodgings catering to foreigners. Of course the agency fees vary with the monthly rent, and clients usually are placed in more expensive apartments.

Eating out can also be difficult, as well as expensive, if you speak only English. Since hotels and restaurants must pay higher wages to employees who are at least bilingual, they must also charge higher prices.

But you plan to prepare you own meals, and surely there must be groceries and markets where someone speaks English. Certainly, there are. But they too must pay employees for their special language skills and pass on the extra cost to the customer.

Sign language is indeed a universal language and is very valuable in many instances. But after you have tried to convey to a pharmacist the need for toothpaste by pantomiming brushing your teeth, you may find yourself moved to learn the local word for toothpaste. These mimes are bound to evoke the often ill-concealed amusement of bystanders and have caused more than one American to flee in embarrassment—without the toothpaste.

C. Robert Temple, in *Americans Abroad*, tells of an informal survey he and a friend made in Madrid among Americans who had lived there for two years and who had no PX or commissary privileges, since they were not connected with the government or the military. Half of those surveyed spoke Spanish (Group A) and half had little or no foreign language competence (Group B). The survey left no doubt that failure to learn Spanish meant a higher cost of living:

	Group A	Group B
Monthly apartment rent	$50–$100	$150–$200
Monthly food cost	$60–$ 80	$100–$150
Monthly servants' wages	$ 8–$ 12	$ 20–$ 30
Entertainment (including movies, restaurants, bull fights, flamenco clubs, nightclubs, concerts, theater)	$90	$175

These were maximum outlays, but the point seems clear: Costs were nearly double for a person who spoke only English.

If you get into the all too frequent legal entanglements, you will find that most representatives of foreign governments speak some English. But red tape often can be untangled—or cut—more quickly if you are able to converse in the native tongue.

This also applies if you are employed by the United States government abroad. Whether you are an ambassador or a clerk-typist, you will come in contact with nationals who do not speak English, and often you will be called upon to help fill out a form, or to explain American foreign policy abroad or desegregation problems at home. Needless to say, the more language facility you have, the easier your job will be.

A native of a Middle Eastern country expressed amazement that Americans would attempt to enter into the affairs of that complex region without a knowledge of Arabic. Admitting that it is one of the most difficult languages to learn, he added that "the Russians who are here speak Arabic fluently."

Every Russian (including the embassy chauffeur) who is sent abroad is rigorously trained in the native language. The Russians know that language skills are vital to the success of any diplomatic mission, and U.S. government administrators are becoming increasingly aware of the fact.

The State Department, particularly, has had a reputation for sending abroad only English-speaking representatives, but it is taking steps rapidly to change the situation.

A foreign service officer, for example, is required to take a foreign language test after he assumes duty with the State Department, although language skills are not required for the initial written examination.

If he can pass a speaking and reading test in any one of the more than thirty languages useful to the department, he receives a salary differential according to his competence.

If he is given an appointment without the language skills, he may not receive more than one promotion until he can pass the language test.

An American working abroad should know the language even if he has been employed because of his knowledge of English (for instance, an interpreter for a foreign firm that does much of its business with British or American firms).

Letters from foreign embassies bear this out. The Brazilian embassy warns: "A good working knowledge of the Portuguese language, the speech of this country, is generally required by those seeking employment. It is considerably more difficult to learn than Spanish."

The embassy of the Federal Republic of Germany, while optimistic about employment opportunities in that country, says: "Ordinarily a good working knowledge of the German language is an indispensable requirement for employment in Germany."

The American Chamber of Commerce in Japan writes: "Inability to speak, understand, or read the Japanese language can be frustrating, and narrows the employment field."

Many American companies sending managers abroad compensate them for language study. In a survey made by the American Management Association, of 31 companies offering some kind of compensation plans, 14 reported that they provided language allowances. Some of these companies included wives and families of employees in the language allowances.

A final, and perhaps most important, reason for learning the language is involved in your reason for wanting to work abroad. If you wish to know the country and its culture intimately, it is vital to know the language. Whether you are attending an informal gathering of your new friends or strolling through the main markets, you can gain a better understanding of the country and its people by knowing the language than from all the books you might read. It is a common experience for an American in a group of foreign friends to have them lapse into their native tongue for side comments that bring gales of laughter. When he asks for a translation so that he can enjoy the story too, the English version offered really isn't funny at all. Something is *always* lost in translation.

It might be added that a foreign language itself often reveals a great deal about the people who speak it. And learning the idioms of a language can provide some delightful experiences. Idiomatic English is often difficult to explain in any other language. Try it sometime with phrases like "on the ball" and "getting a kick out of" something.

How to Learn Another Language

When you have decided you must learn another language, how do you go about it?

There are, of course, many ways. First you must decide what language you are going to learn, which could be a big step in itself.

Then, if you have a talent for languages, you might learn by yourself with a good textbook and a recorded course. Occasionally educational radio or television stations conduct series of language lessons.

You might join a class in an adult education center, and there are many things to be said for this method, particularly if the teacher is competent. It gives you the opportunity not only to hear the language pronounced correctly, but also to learn from the mistakes of your classmates. You may have to wait patiently while the teacher works with a slow learner, but you will also be challenged to your maximum efforts if the class is faster than you are. It is wise to choose a class that emphasizes conversation rather than reading skill.

A third method is to enter one of the many language schools springing up in most major American cities. There you would have a tutor who would proceed at your speed and help you with the more involved grammatical constructions.

A fourth method is recommended only for the very self-confident. You can arrive on foreign soil armed with your two years of high-school or college study of the language and hope that you can "pick up" conversational ability from the people who speak it best. Unfortunately, this takes a great deal of cooperation from the nationals —who, upon learning that you are American, are more likely to try out their English on you.

When one young woman from the Midwest tried out her college French on a Frenchman, he tried determinedly to switch the conversation to English and then complained, "You speak French like an American." While she did not doubt that this was true, she overcame her impulse to apologize and responded, "You speak English like a Frenchman." He was taken aback for a minute, but just as she was beginning to wonder if she had offended him, he burst into laughter and said, "We will help one another. Yes?"

If it is impossible to learn the language before you leave home, you can acquire it by speaking it abroad once you have convinced your foreign contacts that you want to learn it. They are, after all, flattered by your interest and are nearly always helpful. Developing language skills may be the most difficult part of preparing yourself for a job overseas, but it can be most rewarding.

If you want a job abroad, you can—and must—learn to speak the language. If you don't, you might as well keep the job you have.

CHAPTER III

Foreign Customs

One of the first things an American encounters abroad is what the psychologists call "cultural shock." It takes many forms and strikes Americans in varying degrees, but it is ever present. You might meet it on arrival in your dealings with the customs officials—or during your first meal abroad—or it might not strike you for months.

When you arrive on foreign soil, you will be in every sense a "foreigner." Perhaps your response is, "Good! That's what I am going abroad for!" If it is, fine. But you have left behind more than a job that you considered tedious and a daily "ham on rye" for lunch. You have left behind more than friends who tend to get dull at parties and surroundings that have lost their charm.

You have left behind an understanding of street signs, meals served in a familiar order, and people who converse at an accepted distance of two to three feet when they meet on the street. In many countries you will find that your sense of time has also been left at home. In short, you will have exchanged a known way of life for a culture that is indeed foreign to you.

Your "way of life" is something you began learning as a child, when you were taught which things were "right" and which things were definitely "wrong" for a child to do. As you grew up, you learned by observing members of your family and friends in their dealings with one another. You learned not only a way to act, but a way of thinking that is in part purely American and in part purely you. But these are all abstracts with which you must cope.

Let us talk about some specific instances in which you might have to make some adjustments. Suppose you have arrived and gone through customs with a minimum of difficulty. Firmly gripping your suitcase, you ignore the taxi driver who tries to grab it, because you know from the map you have studied so carefully that the hotel is only two blocks away. Now you need only locate the right street and proceed straight for two blocks. You pride yourself on your economy.

The first problem, of course, is the street signs. Assuming you can read the language fluently, you must first find the signs. In some cities they are placed on posts at sidewalk corners as in the United States. In others they stand in the middle of the street. In still others the sign you want may be attached to a building on the street corner where you might find it easily—provided the building isn't set back fifty feet from the street and surrounded by a wall. Of course, some countries have no street signs at all. And in Japan, until the occupation by American forces after World War II, the streets had no names at all.

Your second problem on the way to the hotel might be the discovery that not all streets are straight as they look on the map, and occasionally their names are changed without warning. It would be best to depend on taxis or—if you care to take the risk—public transportation for the first few days.

Air travel, for all its speed and efficiency, is often responsible for at least part of the feeling of strangeness in a new land. When you leave home on a wet winter Monday and by Tuesday afternoon find yourself halfway around the world in searing heat, you simply do not have time to adjust to the change. In the days of sea voyages, travelers had weeks and even months to adjust to leaving home before arriving in a new and strange place.

Another factor contributing to cultural shock is the language difference. You will be surrounded by people who at best speak English with an accent to which your ear must become acclimated. And no matter how fluent you consider yourself in another language, the first sound of voices around you in animated conversation can be frightening. In some countries everyday conversation is conducted in shouts, and you may be convinced that you have stumbled into a verbal battle.

Many foreign customs can quickly change from charming to annoying.

Greeting a friend on the street at home usually means a friendly "Hi, Charlie" or perhaps a more formal handshake. In some European countries a handshake is often merely perfunctory, but in Latin American countries a hearty handshake is followed by an *abrazo,* or embrace, with much shoulder-pounding, and then another handshake.

In some Mediterranean countries (notably Italy) the food is highly seasoned, and a greeting in close quarters can sometimes be tolerated only by taking a deep breath when you see it coming and holding your breath until it is over. To draw away because your friend has had garlic or onions for lunch would be an affront to his naturally cordial nature.

In many countries normal conversation is held with the speakers only six inches apart. Should you draw away, the speaker would automatically close the gap. If you continue to move away, he would almost certainly be offended.

Many of the customs of our society are derived from our Puritan background. Bodily contact is limited, and the blustering "back slapper" is seldom popular.

In other countries, however, bodily contact is commonplace. In crowded public transportation you may find yourself sharing a seat designed for two with two businessmen, a housewife, three children, and a chicken.

You must be prepared for jostling on crowded streets. People of other nations rarely engage in that peculiar American dance in which two people meeting head-on step first to one side and then to the other before one finally stands still and lets the other pass.

Many of the odors you will encounter abroad are delightful and will be part of your lifetime memories, but many will not. Not all countries have municipal garbage disposal. In Arab lands there is usually a narrow sewage trench down the center of the old streets, and when the hot sun of the Middle East blazes down, the odor is something to which you must become accustomed.

Meals can be a strange and wonderful experience abroad if you are willing to try some of the native dishes and to learn native ways with food.

One family arrived at an "out-of-the-way" hotel outside of Vera Cruz, Mexico, at about 1 P.M. and were surprised to find themselves the only customers in a large dining room. The waiter presented them with menus written in Spanish, which they could not read. So each one chose a typewritten line and pointed to it.

The meal that followed lasted nearly two hours and consisted of the same seven courses for each member of the family—all quite unpalatable.

They later discovered what they should have known: It was midsummer and "siesta time," and the food they had been served had been left over from dinner the night before. The custom at the hotel was to serve breakfast about 9 A.M. and the main meal nearly twelve hours later.

Many Americans eating in "out-of-the-way" places choose cooked foods or fresh fruits and vegetables from which a peel or other outer covering can be removed. But don't avoid the local fruits and vegetables completely; they can be truly delicious.

You may prefer to order bottled drinks with your meals, although an American's constant question "Is the water good here?" annoys many people. *They* drink it. Why can't *you?*

In many countries, notably France, it is customary to drink wine at meals. Remember that this is not a sign of sin or moral weakness, but simply a pleasant custom.

Just as you go to another country with preconceived ideas of what you will find, the natives will have preconceived ideas of what you as an American are like.

Just as you may have been told that Germans are good businessmen, that Mexicans are lazy, and that Middle Eastern countries are backward, your foreign counterpart is convinced that you are loud and wear garishly unsuitable clothes, that you expect every foreigner to cheat you, and that you consider all foreigners stupid.

Unfortunately, this is a true picture of some Americans abroad, but you know it isn't true of all Americans. You know that you wouldn't approach a foreigner, slap him on the back, and start asking questions. You know you wouldn't call a new acquaintance by his first name until asked. You know you would be discreet and polite in all circumstances.

But you must be prepared to encounter false impressions from other people and to deal with them as best you can. You might well be prepared for the surprising experience of learning as much about yourself and what is American as you do about the foreigner and his country.

Working Conditions Abroad

As the social customs abroad may be difficult to get used to, so may your working conditions. You may be expected to put in a forty-eight-hour week, and strange hours, at that.

An American engineer working in Elath, at the southernmost tip of Israel, where temperatures soar to 124° F. in the summer, began his work day at 6 A.M. and worked until 8 A.M., when he returned to the hotel for a two-hour "breakfast break." Working again from 10 A.M. to 1 P.M., he had another hour for lunch and rest in the heat of the day, and at 2 P.M. he began his last stint of work.

In Belgium a forty-eight-hour week has been common, but labor-management agreements in many industries have reduced this to forty-five hours (five days of nine hours). Belgium has special protection for women and minors, forbidding dangerous work, additional work at home, and work at night.

In most countries you would work on the Fourth of July and Memorial Day, and in non-Christian countries on Christmas Day. But in European nations paid legal holidays include Assumption Day (August 15), All Saints' Day (November 1), and Pentecost Monday. Labor Day may be celebrated on May 1, not the first Monday after the first Tuesday in September.

In some countries you would be expected to join a union; in others the unions may be part of the political system or nonexistent.

Just as social customs and etiquette vary from country to country, so do business customs.

Air France, the French airline, provides a booklet entitled *Appointment in Europe?* containing helpful hints for anyone dealing with a businessman abroad:

1. Know the title of the person you are addressing, such as Doctor, Professor, or Director, and use the title at all times (without the surname). First names are rarely used, and then only if he suggests it.

2. Be prepared, if you are a man, to shake hands with everybody, including his secretary and any business associates he calls in.

3. Be on time, particularly in the northern European countries. In the southern countries, where life in general is more relaxed, a delay is of less consequence. In fact, you may have to wait.

4. Dress conservatively. If you are a man and accustomed to wearing a hat, do so, but be prepared to tip it a great deal.

5. If you are invited to lunch, accept graciously and don't grab for the check or offer to "go Dutch." He expects to pay when it is his invitation and may be offended otherwise.

Although a businessman in Europe may expect to get right to the point, in the Orient or Middle East it may take from three hours to three weeks of "small talk" and inquiries into the health of innumerable relatives before the business at hand comes into the conversation at all.

Perhaps one of the best available pictures of the varying social and business customs you might encounter abroad is contained in *The Overseas American*.[1] The authors have made their point by using contrasting concepts of time.

"If an American is invited to an eight o'clock dinner, the chances are he will arrange to get there between five to fifteen minutes after eight. His Scandanavian friend will have arrived on the dot of eight, very likely carrying a gift. A Latin may politely come to the same dinner at nine, some Ethiopians might come even later, and a Javanese, having courteously accepted the invitation in order to avoid any loss of face on the host's part, may not show up at all."

The *Wall Street Journal,* in a 1965 article about American companies hiring local managers abroad, says:

> In Ethiopia, for instance, an American executive of the bustling efficient type that might make a big splash at home is likely to rank low in the eyes of local businessmen; a local manager, on the other hand, will know instinctively that the way to impress Ethiopian businessmen is to maintain an unhurried, deliberate air at all times. . . . U.S. executives who do take jobs in foreign countries not infrequently face problems arising from the inability of their families to adjust to the new life. Wives may feel isolated and unhappy at distant corporate outposts.

"The drinking problem alone among wives overseas can be a big concern," says Robert A. Staub, a management consultant active in recruiting for overseas jobs. He recalls one executive's wife from Nebraska "who became lonely in the Far East and drank so much that her husband's employer had to bring the couple back to the U.S."

While this is a tragic commentary, it serves to warn the unwary of the consequences of cultural shock resulting from a drastic change in social and business customs.

Two of the most valuable characteristics for taking cultural shock in stride are: *a ready adaptability* to ways that at the outset seem strange and, even more important, *a sense of humor,* which can be the single most useful item in your mental luggage.

[1] *The Overseas American,* Harlan Cleveland, Gerard J. Mangone, and John Clarke Adams, McGraw-Hill, 1960.

CHAPTER IV

Work Permits

Doing anything out of the ordinary these days seems to require yards of red tape and stacks of legal paper work, and going abroad to work is no exception. The usual channels of tourist information have provided you with forms to fill out for your passport, entry visas, and health certificates. You have raised your right hand in the presence of witnesses and sworn to uphold the Constitution, and your doctor has stamped your health certificate to assure the authorities that he has indeed filled you with the necessary vaccines, antitoxins, and serums.

But before you pack your bags and head for your exciting adventure working abroad, one document is required by most countries, on which may hinge your success or even your entry into a foreign country—a work permit.

A work permit will not of itself assure you of a job, nor will it insure that, when you have secured a job, you will do it well and be happy at it. It will, however, show the immigration officials that you have the permission of that country's government to enter and to be employed there.

In most cases, work permits must be obtained before you leave home, since they must be shown upon arrival. Most countries that require permits do so to keep outsiders from flooding the labor market and taking jobs that might be held by nationals. Permits are normally issued freely to persons having skills that are not readily available within the country. If you have already obtained a job that will take you abroad, your employer will usually make arrangements for a work permit.

Since labor conditions vary from country to country, a sampling of foreign work-permit regulations follows. It might be wise, however, to consult the consulate of the country in which you are going to work for more specific details, as requirements may be affected by a fluctuating labor situation.

It should go without saying that diplomatic considerations must be remembered. Factors of foreign policy may make it unwise—if not impossible—for you as an American to consider working in certain countries.

Argentina

It is a common practice in Argentina for foreigners to enter on a tourist visa, obtain employment, and use this as proof to the immigration authorities that they are self-supporting. They can thus obtain a permanent residence permit, which is usually a prerequisite to obtaining an identity document, "Cedula de Identitad," issued by the federal police. An alien may obtain a permanent residence permit by applying to one of the Argentine consulates before leaving the United States, although this usually takes longer.

Australia

Although it is sometimes possible to work in Australia with only a passport and tourist visa, it is usually necessary to enter with migrant status. Entry papers permitting work in Australia are issued readily to American or Canadian citizens of European descent who meet certain age requirements and are of sound health and good character. Write to:

    Australian Consulate-General
    636 Fifth Avenue
    New York, N.Y. 10020

Austria

Foreigners who intend to seek employment in Austria must have an employment permit and a labor permit. The employment permit, like most work permits, must be applied for by your prospective employer before you leave for Austria. The Austrian consular authorities will issue a visa on the basis of this permit. After you have arrived in Austria, you or your employer may apply for your labor permit, which constitutes actual permission to start work. The employment and labor permits are valid for a year, but they may be extended by the provincial or local Labor Exchange.

Belgium

Because there is a shortage of qualified manpower in Belgium, work permits are relatively easy to obtain. More than 500 American firms have plants or subsidiaries there. For most salaried jobs, the employer arranges for a work permit. If, however, you wish to work in Belgium on your own, you must take five steps:

1. An application for a visa must be submitted in quadruplicate to the nearest Embassy or Career Consulate.

2. At the same time, a medical certificate must be submitted, including a statement that you have no contagious disease and are not likely to require hospitalization for any illness in the foreseeable future.

3. A certificate issued by your local police department must be submitted, stating that you have had no police record for the past five years.

4. An application for a professional card (carte professionelle) must be submitted in triplicate.

5. You must also be ready to produce references and proof of your financial standing.

If you have already arranged for a job in Belgium, and your employer will secure a work permit for you, send him a police certificate, three recent passport-size photographs, complete personal data (including date and place of birth, residence in the United States, and nationality) and a medical certificate written in French or Dutch on the doctor's letterhead.

Processing of an application usually takes four weeks, so it is well to make arrangements for leaving for Belgium only after you have secured your work permit.

For legal forms or for more information write to:

Belgian Embassy
3330 Garfield Street, N.W.
Washington, D.C.

or

Belgian Chamber of Commerce in the United States, Inc.
50 Rockefeller Plaza
New York, N.Y. 10017

Bermuda

Work permits are not required in Bermuda, but employment opportunities for aliens are few since they may not be employed unless no Bermudian is qualified to fill the position. Opportunities for aliens exist in specialized fields—teaching, nursing, secretarial work, and accounting—and it is relatively easy to obtain hotel work.

You may go to Bermuda on a one-way ticket if you or your employer will deposit the cost of a return ticket with the Bermuda Board of Immigration.

For more information, write to:

> The Bermuda Trade Development Board
> 620 Fifth Avenue
> New York, N.Y. 10020

Brazil

Brazil, in spite of its immense territory and undeveloped resources, does not offer great employment possibilities. Because of the relatively low wage scale and the Brazilian law governing the employment of aliens, the embassy strongly warns against going to Brazil to work without having obtained a job in advance.

To work in Brazil, you must first be admitted to the country as an immigrant or permanent resident. You can enter Brazil to work on a temporary basis only if you have a legal contract. (Tourists are not allowed to work in Brazil under any circumstances, and no one is permitted to enter the country to look for a job.)

To get a permanent visa, you must assure the consular officer in the United States that you can maintain yourself and your dependents and that you are free of communicable disease. When you arrive in Brazil with a permanent visa, you must register with the local police and obtain an identity card.

Canada

If you are going to Canada as a nonimmigrant, you must obtain written permission to work from the immigration officer, who will first check with the National Employment Service to see that no Canadian resident is qualified and able to accept the position you seek. Only if you have qualifications much in demand and in short supply are you likely to obtain permission.

If you wish to work in Canada only for a temporary period, write to the Canadian Immigration Officer nearest to your intended destination for permission to work. Unless you are highly qualified in your field and the services you offer are in demand in Canada, it is unlikely that your request will be granted.

Czechoslovak Socialist Republic

Czechoslovakia has no law governing work permits. You may request work in connection with an application for permanent residence, and perhaps in connection with a prolonged visit. Each request is handled individually on its merits, although a person who is already in Czechoslovakia is more apt to receive permission to work, since he is more likely to have found suitable employment.

Costa Rica

You may apply for a resident's visa in Costa Rica either before you leave home or after arriving on a tourist visa. You must submit:

1. A notarized application stating your reasons for residence (accompanied by a $2 fee).
2. A certificate of financial solvency given by a resident of Costa Rica.
3. A legal birth certificate, a "no police record" document, and a medical certificate including smallpox vaccination, blood test, and lung examination.

The application must be signed by three witnesses and by local authorities (usually the county clerk) and the nearest Costa Rican Consul General. An authenticated translation in Spanish, certified by the consul and by the Ministry of Foreign Affairs, must accompany these documents. All documents must be sent for processing to the Consejo de Immegracio, San José, Costa Rica. When they have been approved, you will be issued a resident's visa. The fee is $25.

Denmark

A work permit in Denmark is valid only for the specific job for which it is granted. You may obtain an application blank by writing to:

The Danish Embassy
3200 Whitehaven Street, N.W.
Washington, D.C. 20008

or to the Royal Danish Consulate General at:

18 East 48th Street New York, N.Y.	360 North Michigan Avenue Chicago, Illinois
291 World Trade Center Ferry Building San Francisco, California	Suite 704, Tishman Building 3440 Wilshire Boulevard Los Angeles, California

When you have filled out the application form, it should be sent
directly to:

Chief of Police (Rigspolitichefen)
Aliens Department
Anker Heegaardsgade 5
Copenhagen V, Denmark

Dominican Republic

Citizens of the United States and of other countries may work in
the Dominican Republic in any enterprise, industrial or commercial,
after they have entered the country. To be permitted entry you must
have a valid passport and a visa obtained from a diplomatic or
consular civil servant of the Dominican Republic.

Finland

To work in Finland, you must have a permit issued by a Finnish
diplomatic or consular officer in the United States. The visa and work-
permit applications must be submitted in triplicate, with three passport photographs, a valid passport, and a statement from your employer in Finland. The application is then sent to Helsinki to the
Ministry of Foreign Affairs for approval. The fee for a work permit
is $2, and processing the application usually takes three to four weeks.
No health or vaccination certificates are required for entry into Finland.

France

Working for an American firm in France does not require a work permit. To work for a French firm you must apply for one, unless you qualify for the student visa, which allows you to remain in France for twelve months.

Since French law governing aliens living and working in France is complex, it is most important to check with the consulate about current regulations. The French Chamber of Commerce states, somewhat enigmatically, that "in the present period of full employment the regulations are applied sympathetically." But it goes on to stress that penalties for remaining in France for more than three months without applying for a residence permit or for failing to renew a permit are fairly heavy: a fine of from $80 to $400 and from ten days' to two months' imprisonment.

Work permits are granted only to employers, who must register all foreign workers within twenty-four hours of hiring them. The employee must first have a residence permit, and all applicants must pass medical examinations. Since permits are granted only for specific jobs in specific locations, an alien may not change jobs before the expiration of the given "undertaking" for which his employment has been approved.

Work permits are issued by:

Services de Main d'Oeuvre du Ministre du Travail
391 Rue de Vaurigard
Paris, France

Procedures for nonsalaried workers involve four different kinds of work permits, depending on the duration of the residence permit. If you fall into this category, by all means check with the consulate or with:

French Chamber of Commerce
250 West 57th Street
New York, N.Y.

Germany

An American entering Germany with the intention to work must first register with the police to obtain a residence permit. This permit, with a statement from his employer, is submitted to the local Landes-arbeitsamt (Labor office), which issues the work permit. If you intend to stay in Germany for more than a year, you must obtain a visa from the German Consulate in the United States. Residence and work permits for Germany are fairly easy to obtain and usually take only a few days.

Great Britain

The British government, while most tolerant in issuing work permits, warns that Great Britain does not offer scope for any large-scale foreign immigration. Because of a shortage of domestic workers, permits are usually granted freely to aliens without children for work in private households and residential catering establishments. Permits also are issued for unskilled workers in the hotel and catering industry from March to the end of October. Few other opportunities exist for unskilled workers, but semi-skilled or skilled workers may obtain permission to work in some industries and services if they can give documentary evidence of their skills.

A permit must be secured by the employer before he can offer a job to an alien. He then sends the permit to the prospective employee, who must present it at the port of arrival with his passport. Without these papers, entry may be refused.

Greece

Employment by Greek firms is restricted to Greek citizens, except in extraordinary instances when a special work permit is granted by the Greek Ministry of Labor. It is possible, of course, to work for the U.S. government or for an American industrial firm with offices in Greece.

India

In order to work in India, you must have the prior approval of the Indian government. This permission is applied for by the sponsoring organization or institution.

Iran

No employer in Iran may employ an alien without permission from the Minister of Labor. Permission will be granted provided that no

Iranian national has the skill and experience to do the job, and provided that the alien does not work for lower wages than those an employer would have to pay a national of Iran to obtain the same services.

The work permit will show the kind of work to be done, the employer's name, and the province in which the alien is to be employed. The employer must also submit the alien's qualifications, the conditions of work, and the reasons for his appointment. It might be added that, even in the case of technical experts, permission is limited to the length of time required to train an Iranian national to do the job.

Ireland

To work in Ireland, you must have a work permit issued to your employer by the Minister for Industry and Commerce.

Italy

The same rules for alien workers apply in Italy as in most of the other member countries of the European Economic Community, except that a work permit is not quite so easy to obtain. When applying for a work permit, you must be able to prove that you will not be holding a job which might put or keep an Italian out of work. Generally, Americans may not work for Italian firms, but they may be employed by American companies active in Italy.

Japan

If you should go to Japan on a tourist visa (60 days) and wished to extend it to a commercial (or three-year) visa, it might be necessary for you to leave the country for an indefinite period before you could re-enter. The American Chamber of Commerce in Japan states that "even though some Americans might agree to work on the Japanese salary scale, the income is not sufficient to maintain even a minimum standard of living for an American."

Mexico

Technicians or specialists in services that cannot be provided locally may be able to obtain "immigration working papers" in Mexico. Executives, directors, managers, superintendents, or heads of firms may also be permitted to work upon application by the prospective employer to the Mexican Immigration authorities. Tourists and students are not authorized to take even temporary employment.

The Netherlands

Work permits in The Netherlands relate to specific jobs. The first step, therefore, is to get a job. Work permits are then issued either to the employer or the employee by the district labor office for the area in which the business is located.

New Zealand

New Zealand is one of the few countries that make it quite easy, and inexpensive, to obtain work permits. For a visa fee of $2, an American can enter with permission to work. The processing may take time, however, and it is well to apply as far in advance as possible. The government also requires that, upon arrival, you register as an alien, a requirement of many countries, including the United States. Application to live permanently in New Zealand should be made to the nearest New Zealand overseas representative, or to the Secretary of Labour, Box 6310, Wellington, New Zealand. If at all possible, such application should be made in person.

Norway

An alien who wishes to seek employment in Norway should obtain a work permit in advance. Application may be sent either to the nearest Norwegian consulate or direct to:

> Norwegian State Alien Office
> Statens Utlendingskontor
> Drammensveien 20
> Oslo, Norway

A work permit, usually granted for an initial period of six months, can be extended indefinitely. If, however, you should decide to look for employment after arriving in the country, you can apply to the nearest police authority for residence and work permits.

Panama

The only requirement for obtaining work in Panama is a resident visa. Application is made through a local lawyer and must be accompanied by police, health, and birth certificates and a deposit of $250.

Philippines

A visa for an already hired employee may be authorized by the Commissioner of Immigration when requested by a Philippine employer, although such requests are rare. Permission will be granted only if there is no Filipino able and willing to perform the work.

Portugal

In order to avoid unemployment, Portuguese law requires that a foreigner seeking employment make prior arrangements with an employer. The employer, in turn, must file an application with the Department of Labor, stating the reasons for employing a foreign skilled worker rather than a Portuguese.

American Samoa

Samoa is a U.S. possession and does not issue work permits. American Samoan nationals are employed in most positions, and only a few professionals and highly skilled technicians are employed from the United States.

Spain

You must have a work permit to be employed in Spain. Your prospective employer makes application at the provincial office of the Ministry of Labor. His request, with the conditions of employment and job specifications, is made public, and the permit is granted if no qualified Spanish citizen applies for the job. A small fee is charged for the permit, and it must be renewed yearly.

South Africa

It is necessary for Americans, though not for Canadians, to have a residence permit in order to work in South Africa. Each member of the family must fill out an application or have one filled out for him, regardless of age. Application forms may be obtained from:

Consulate General of South Africa
655 Madison Avenue
New York, N.Y.

When you arrive in South Africa, you must be able to show that you have enough money to keep you until you find work.

Sweden

After you have received a concrete offer of employment in Sweden, you must apply for a labor permit. It may take some time for the permit to be granted. You may get application forms from the Swedish Embassy in Washington or from your nearest consular representative. Applications should be sent directly to:

> State Alien Commission
>   (Statens Utlanningskommission)
> Birgerjarlstorg 5
> Stockholm, Sweden

If you plan to stay in Sweden for more than three months, you will need a residence permit, which you may get either from the above address or at the local Swedish police station.

Thailand

No work permits are required in Thailand, but you must conform to immigration regulations and obtain a permit to live in that country. For more information write to the Royal Thai Embassy in Washington.

Trinidad and Tobago

First preference for jobs is given to citizens of Trinidad and Tobago, but if you have special qualifications you may be given permission to work if no citizen is available. Your employer must apply to the Chief Immigration Officer for your entry and residence permission for the period of your employment, and he must satisfy the authorities that your employment is necessary. The conditions sometimes imposed requiring the training of a national to succeed you might give you an uneasy feeling if you were going there to perform a new job.

Turkey

Application for a permit to work in Turkey should be sent to the Turkish Consulate General, 50 Rockefeller Plaza, New York, N.Y. 10020, or 53 West Jackson Boulevard, Chicago, Illinois 60604. After you have filled out the papers, ask for the date and number of the transmittal letter to the authorities in Turkey. You may either wait for your reply in the United States or go to Turkey and check with the authorities about your pending application. (United States citizens may enter Turkey for a stay of up to three months without a visa.) Usually it takes some time for work-permit applications to be processed.

Venezuela

Persons going to Venezuela on business or under contract must have a "transient visa." This is valid for one year, may be extended for a second year, and then may be changed to a resident visa. You must present the following documents to the Consul in person:

1. Valid passport.
2. Smallpox vaccination certificate.
3. General health certificate.
4. Police "good conduct" certificate.
5. Letter from employer stating purpose and length of trip.
6. One profile and five front-view photographs.
7. Medical certificate based on X ray showing you are free of pulmonary diseases.

Virgin Islands

Since the Virgin Islands are a United States possession, no work permit is required. If you plan to go there, however, you should take your birth or naturalization certificate to establish your date of birth and U.S. citizenship, especially if you plan to work for the government. The government of the Virgin Islands provides for partial reimbursement of travel expenses for you and your family if you accept employment there.

The foregoing is the most recent information available on work-permit requirements in some of the countries in which you might seek employment. It is always a good idea to check with the foreign consulates in this country for any revisions in the regulations given, or with those of countries not specifically mentioned. The addresses of the major consulates are listed in the Appendix.

CHAPTER V

Help from American and Foreign Consulates

It may be said at the outset that the United States government can give you very little aid in getting a job abroad with a private firm. It can, of course, give you much information about government employment, which will be dealt with in a later chapter.

The American consulates abroad, however, may be of great help should you find yourself in a country in which you would like to spend more time. It would certainly be well to check with the consulate, for example, for possible job openings or for information about local regulations governing Americans.

The American consulates abroad strongly suggest that you register with them if you decide to stay longer than an average tourist. They would like to know where you can be reached if necessary. And, although you certainly don't intend to get into trouble, legal or otherwise, it might help to be dealing with consular officials who at least recognize your name if you do.

Probably the best information about living and working abroad can be obtained before you board your plane or ship. Most countries maintain embassies in Washington, D.C., and many have consulates in the principal U.S. cities.

Letters to these embassies or consulates (see Appendix C for embassy addresses) will bring responses varying from a brief statement of alien rights to more detailed explanations of monetary systems and laws governing household pets. They also may give you some idea of the current job situation for aliens and even leads on job openings.

A letter to the consulate of the country of your choice should be your first order of business—*before* you pick up your travel brochures. The response will tell you surely whether your vague dream of working in a given country can ever become a reality.

Below are condensations of replies to letters to consulates, embassies, and chambers of commerce that will give you an idea of the kind of information you might expect to receive.

Australia

This country can be a real "land of opportunity" for Americans looking for employment abroad. Not only is there no language difficulty, but jobs are plentiful and quite easy to find. There are jobs for skilled labor and many for people with lesser skills, not only in the major cities of Sydney and Melbourne, but in the "outlands," if you prefer avoiding crowds.

Although there has been a housing shortage in Australia, nearly 80,000 homes and apartments are being built annually, but rentals are often high.

If you plan to stay in Australia for more than two years, you might check the Commonwealth's Passage Assistance Scheme. The government will, after your arrival in Australia, pay $160 toward the passage for each adult and a lesser amount for each child. You must, however, sign an agreement to return the money if you or any member of your family leaves before the two years are up.

While the wage rates may seem low, the cost of living in Australia is low, too. Income tax rates are high because of the many health and social benefits, but should you stay for less than six months, your tax contribution would be refunded.

All aliens in Australia are required to register and are penalized for failure to do so.

The Australian Consulate General will also tell you about the climate, system of government, transportation, duty regulations, and whether or not your electrical appliances will work in Australia.

Austria

The Austrian Information Service (31 East 69th Street, New York, N.Y.) will send you a list of regulations governing the employment of foreigners, information about summer and temporary work for students (more about that in Chapter XV), and a list of principal Austrian newspapers carrying employment advertisements.

Belgium

At present, several hundred thousand aliens are working in Belgium, but generally speaking, jobs are not as readily available in Belgium as in the United States, and salaries and wages are considerably lower. For more information write to:

American Embassy, Shell Building
60 Rue Ravenstein
Brussels, Belgium

or

Industrial Information Service
Belgian Consulate General
New York, N.Y.

Bermuda

A letter to the Bermuda Trade Development Board (620 Fifth Avenue, New York, N.Y.) will bring you a list of the larger hotels, some of which employ aliens, and information on the cost of living, on schools, and on housing, including a list of real estate agents in Bermuda. Although prices in Bermuda are generally slightly higher than in the metropolitan areas of the eastern United States, personal finances are balanced by the fact that there is no income tax and, in fact, no tax of any kind except a very small parish tax on property.

Brazil

In a memorandum regarding employment of Americans in Brazil, the Chamber of Commerce for Brazil points out that there are restrictions on occupations that can be followed by noncitizens. The Constitution reserves to Brazilian citizens the practice of professions—medicine, dentistry, engineering, and architecture. There is no field for American trained nurses, principally because of the low wage scale. A few American teachers are employed in the few American schools in Brazil, most of which are denominational.

São Paulo is given as an example of climate, housing and rental facilities ("houses and apartments that are available are going for three or four times their normal rental"), schools, churches, and average living expenses.

Jobs are available for aliens in Brazil, but two thirds of all employees in commerce or industry must be Brazilians. Foreigners may not be employed as stevedores or dock or harbor workers, except where authorized.

Chile

Anyone remaining in Chile for more than two months must register and obtain identification and residence cards. Only after a year may aliens apply for a permanent residence permit. Mining and construction companies provide most of the work for Americans in Chile.

Costa Rica

Costa Rica welcomes qualified men and women who wish to work in any of the many lines of service and production. More than 3,000 Americans live and work in Costa Rica, and the embassy says, "We are grateful for their contribution."

The policy of the Ministry of Labor and Social Welfare is to give assistance to all immigrants; preference is given to those who can teach Costa Ricans new skills, crafts, or professions or who establish new sources of jobs.

Denmark

Officials at the Danish Embassy, while warning that they cannot help to get jobs in Denmark, will provide a list of the leading Danish newspapers that run help-wanted ads.

Officials at the American Embassy in Denmark report that housing is scarce and rigidly controlled. "Available apartments and houses are often far from ideal and, in general, only the higher-priced ones have plumbing and kitchen appliances up to American standards. Heating costs are always borne by the tenant and can be quite high because of the long winters and the size of the rooms in the older houses."

Foreigners who have been in Denmark more than three months may participate in the public illness insurance program for a moderate monthly fee, which insures free medical treatment by panel physicians and other benefits.

Finland

The Embassy of Finland will send on request information on opportunities for students and on trainee programs (see Chapter XV), on regulations governing entry to Finland, and on the amount of money and other commodities that may be brought into the country.

France

The French Consulate in the United States states that "Americans in France who hope to find full or part-time work should be warned before they leave of the difficulties to be encountered." A *carte de sejour* is required for anyone staying for more than 90 days and is issued only on evidence of adequate means of support (a regular job or student status).

Anyone arriving in the country without a definite job contract with a reputable employer must be prepared for a long job hunt that may prove disappointing. An experienced bilingual shorthand-typist will have the least difficulty in finding a job, but above and below this level the situation is not easy. "It is practically impossible for a foreigner to find ordinary clerical or office work."

The one exception is the opportunity for a girl to live with a French family, exchanging housework and child care for board and lodging. This is open to young women between the ages of eighteen and thirty who will stay in France for at least six months. Since there are obvious risks of abuse, the French Consulate suggests arranging for this kind of situation through:

Accueil Familial de Jeunes Étrangers
23 Rue de Cherche-Midi
Paris VI, France

The French Consulate ends its letter (which it mimeographs to send out to the thousands of college graduates who want to work in Paris) as follows:

"In short, the employment fields of France are barren as far as young Americans are concerned. Anyone setting out, unprepared, to earn his living there must be prepared for a difficult, bleak adventure."

We shall speak later about work opportunities for students in Paris.

Germany

Germany offers many career opportunities to young people and is doing its best to attract them to its labor market. The housing situation is good, and many American servicemen have remained in Germany to work for American or German firms after their discharge.

If you would like to work in Germany, you might write to:

Zentralstelle für Arbeitsvermittlung und Vermittlungsausgleich
6 Frankfurt-am-Main

Eschersheimer Landstrasse 1–7
Germany

This office will help you to get a job in Germany as well as give you a general idea of the employment situation.

The U.S. Department of Commerce has a booklet entitled "Residence and Business Rights of Aliens in the Federal Republic of Germany." You may have a copy by sending 10 cents to the:

U.S. Department of Commerce
Bureau of International Commerce
Washington, D.C. 20230

Great Britain

The British Information Services has many leaflets available for anyone interested in working in Great Britain. Among them are:

"Employment of Foreigners in the United Kingdom" (ID 1472), with information about employment with American and British firms, salaries, and regulations governing aliens.

"Setting Up Residence in the United Kingdom" (ID 873), with information about the cost of living, social services, and importing household effects, house plants, and motor vehicles, among many other subjects.

"Costs of Living in Britain" (ID 1014), with detailed information about currency and rate of exchange, taxes on goods, food, rent, and household expenses, and costs of personal items, entertainment, vacations, and transportation.

"Advice to Teachers Who Wish to Teach in Great Britain and Northern Ireland" (ID 774), with information about schools, interviews, and teacher exchange.

These leaflets may be obtained by writing to:

British Information Services, Economics Division
845 Third Avenue
New York, N.Y. 10022

Greece

The Greek Embassy, while warning that it is not usually possible for aliens to work in Greece, says that employment might be found with an American firm. For further information, the embassy suggests that you write to the U.S. Department of Commerce in Washington, D.C., or to the Commercial Attaché of the United States Embassy in Athens. For employment with U.S. government missions in Greece, it is necessary to apply to the appropriate governmental agency in the United States.

If you are interested in teaching in one of three American-operated schools in Greece, write to:

Teacher Placement
Near East College Association
548 Fifth Avenue
New York, N.Y. 10017

Schools are also operated for dependents of American military personnel in Greece; for information, write to the U.S. Defense Department.

Iran

The Iran American Chamber of Commerce publishes a booklet of regulations and laws concerning the encouragement and protection of foreign investment and the employment of aliens in Iran. The laws are quite specific, and if you would like to work in Iran you must have a copy of the booklet, which can be obtained by writing to:

Secretariat
Iran American Chamber of Commerce
Harwood Building
Scarsdale, N.Y.

Israel

Israel is a young, vital nation with a great need for workers in professional and technical fields. Housing conditions, which have not been good, are rapidly improving. General conditions are not easy even now, and taxes are high: "Israel is a land of contrasts. We have the lowest spot on the earth's surface—the Dead Sea—and the highest tax rate."

Broad employment opportunities exist for professionals, however, including engineers (mechanical, civil, electrical, and electronic), food technologists, physicians, educational and clinical psychologists, social workers, and teachers.

For more information, write to:

Committee on Manpower Opportunities in Israel
515 Park Avenue
New York, N.Y. 10017

It must be noted, however, that under Israeli law anyone entering Israel on an immigration visa is subject to military service, regardless of nationality. This includes men between the ages of eighteen and twenty-nine, unmarried women between eighteen and twenty-six, and medical doctors who are under thirty-eight. If a doctor wishes to leave the country before completing military service, he must have authorization from the Ministry of Defense. If you meet the above requirements and do indeed become a member of the Israel Defense Army, you risk losing your right to protection by the United States government.

Italy

Although jobs may be obtained in Italy, they are few and far between. If you do obtain a job, you will have the same civil rights as Italian citizens. You may get a list of American companies with subsidiaries in Italy from the:

United States Embassy
Via Vittorio Veneto 119
Rome, Italy

Japan

The large majority of Americans employed in Japan are recruited in the United States and sent to Japan by their companies or by the U.S. government. Pay is relatively low, and income taxes are high, but recently there has been a labor shortage. Resident aliens must register with the police and can claim nearly all the rights of citizens except political rights.

The American Chamber of Commerce in Japan offers a booklet entitled "Living Conditions in Japan," which may be had for 10 cents from the Bureau of International Commerce, Washington, D.C. It covers entrance and exit requirements, customs procedures, cost of living, taxation, health conditions and medical facilities, institutions and language, transportation and communications, and government representation, as well as a list of selected reading.

Mexico

In addition to a list of regulations governing aliens in Mexico, the embassy will send you lists of employment agencies in Mexico City and of Mexican attorneys who will help you get immigration working papers.

Netherlands

You must have a permit if you intend to stay in The Netherlands more than three months. A work license is also required if you have paid employment.

New Zealand

Nearly the same conditions apply to New Zealand as to Australia. Aliens in New Zealand may also buy and sell real and personal property.

The embassy will send you a copy of a brochure entitled "Information on Employment for United States and Canadian Citizens Who Wish to Emigrate to New Zealand," which covers the general employment position, housing, national services, and general opportunities for women, as well as specific opportunities in specialized fields.

Norway

Generally speaking, it is not easy for foreigners to obtain work in Norway. According to the Norwegian Labor Directorate, job opportunities are best for seasonal farm workers (May to September), chambermaids and waitresses during tourist season, practical nurses, nurses' aids, kitchen helpers in hospitals and other institutions, domestics in private homes, skilled workers, and women workers in various fields.

In some communities it may be difficult to find suitable lodgings if not provided by the employer.

Peru

Although only 20 per cent of the employees in a profession or industry in Peru may be aliens, those who do get jobs have the same civil rights and duties as citizens, but resident aliens pay a small alien tax.

Philippines

The Philippines turns out annually such a great number of graduates in various fields, and the labor force is growing so fast in relation to new employment opportunities, that it is usually necessary to fill jobs from the ranks of Filipino citizens.

Portugal

Foreigners in Portugal may not establish or buy factories without special government authorization. In some cases, aliens may not be employed without a license. Doctors may work in Portugal only in the case of urgent needs for public health services, scientific research, or teaching.

South Africa

Doctors, nurses, technicians, and miners are in short supply in South Africa, and job opportunities in these fields are nearly unlimited. Though the wage scale varies considerably, the pay in general is high and the cost of living lower than in the United States. The standard of living is high, and most people have servants. Political restrictions on civil rights make it inadvisable for an American Negro to apply for work, because of the common practice of *apartheid,* or separation of races.

Spain

Competition for jobs in Spain is strongest in the cities of Madrid and Barcelona. You must have a labor contract and a professional identity card issued by the labor office.

Sweden

When you have gone through the legalities of work and residence permits in Sweden, you are encouraged to join a union to make sure you receive the high pay that nationals receive. Living standards are very high, and wages are among the highest in Europe.

The Swedish Embassy will send you on request a reprint from an annual report of the Swedish National Market Board, which includes information regarding aliens and work permits, and private employment services.

Switzerland

The Swiss Embassy warns that at present and in the foreseeable future Switzerland will not grant work or residence permits to foreigners. On the contrary, the number of foreign workers and residents must be reduced, as the economy can no longer support the great influx of aliens.

Thailand

The following trades are reserved to their nationals: making images of Buddha, barbering, hairdressing, and typesetting; work in the nielloware or salt industries or in rice cultivation; and the operation of motorcycles, motorcars, or buses for public transport. For any other work except government service, you will be welcome, provided you conform to immigration regulations, which require a permit to reside in Thailand.

Turkey

Turkey restricts even more trades and professions to Turkish nationals: peddlers, musicians, photographers, hairdressers, typesetters, brokers, and workers in suit, hat, and shoe production; buyers in commodity and stock exchanges; dealers in state monopoly goods; interpreters and guides for tourists; permanent and temporary workers in transportation, irrigation (and generally in water supply), heating, and communications; land-loading and -unloading workers; drivers and assistant drivers; laborers; janitors, engineers and guards in all institutions, commercial buildings, bathhouses, coffee houses, bars, dance halls, and nightclubs; nightclub singers and dancers; veterinarians; and chemists.

Airplane pilots and engineers may work as aliens in Turkey only after securing a special permit.

U.S.S.R.

It is generally agreed that too many hidden restrictions exist to make it advisable for Americans to work in the Soviet Union, except as employees of the U.S. government or news media.

Venezuela

The Embassy of Venezuela offers a mimeographed list of regulations governing foreigners and also a list of United States firms operating in that country.

Venezuela is undergoing rapid industrialization and has many building programs. Many American companies are involved in construction, mining, and oil production. Although 75 per cent of the jobs must be held by nationals, openings exist for women as well as men. Women are needed as clerk-typists, secretaries, teachers, and nurses. It has been said that the turnover for women is great because many of them marry Americans employed in Venezuela.

The Embassy reports that when highly specialized technicians are needed either by the Venezuelan government or by private companies, they are hired abroad. The chances of getting employment in Venezuela depend on factors prevailing anywhere in the world: experience, training, past record, ability to fill a given position, knowledge of the language, and even luck.

The embassy offers a statement of living conditions in Venezuela, such as housing ("apartments are plentiful in Caracas"), domestic help ("a maid and cook are considered essential even for couples without children and earn $65 to $85 monthly"), education ("schools are free on the primary, secondary, and even university level, and standards of education are high even in small towns"), churches, medical care, health, climate, transportation, recreation, clothing, and taxes.

Although the cost of living is about as high as in any large city of the United States, it is more than offset by lower taxes, especially in the case of resident foreigners. Imported foods are naturally higher in price than domestic foods, but the best grades of domestic beef sell generally for from 55 cents to 75 cents per pound. Milk is 30 cents a quart, but gasoline is 11 or 12 cents per gallon.

In conclusion, most embassies and consulates will be helpful in response to your inquiry about working in a given country.

A final note: If you or your parents are naturalized American citizens and you plan to return to your country of origin, it would be wise to check with the consulate about your military status in that country. Many countries expect you to serve military duty if you or your parents have ever been subjects.

Pay Scales Abroad

While some people have both the interest and the financial resources to go abroad for unpaid volunteer service, it is most likely that your motive in earning a paycheck will fall into one of two categories. You may want to be able to live abroad without dipping into your savings, or you may hope to earn a nest egg to pay off a mortgage, educate yourself or your children, or care for aging parents. Or perhaps you would like to do both.

The category you fall into determines the kind of job you should accept overseas.

If you hope to build up savings, you will be better off working for an American employer, either the United States government or a private firm engaged in the oil, mining, or construction industries. On the other hand, if your principal interest is in living abroad, you may be willing to accept the smaller salaries paid by foreign firms.

Pay for Employees of the United States Government

Whether you work as an employee of the State or Commerce Department or as a civilian employee of one of the military services, your salary will be governed by Civil Service scales.

Generally you will earn up to 25 per cent more for working overseas than in the same job at home.

Salaries of State and Commerce Department employees under Civil Service are determined by a grade level, which varies with skills and seniority under Civil Service. You would be classified at Grade 9, for example, if you could type 50 words per minute, take shorthand at 96 words per minute, and had six years of office experience and two years of continued secretarial experience. You would receive $4,575 a year as a base salary, with annual pay raises of $155 if you performed your job satisfactorily.

The pay range for civilian employees of the military is much the same as for other government employees abroad (with the exception of Foreign Service officers). Pay rates range from about $3,820 to $4,110 for stenographers, to $6,675 to $14,565 for auditors or accountants.

If you were to enter the Foreign Service (we will deal later with requirements and opportunities), your salary would be determined by your classification. It can range up to $20,000 for a career ambassador. The salary range in the Foreign Service by classification is as follows:

Class 1	$18,975–$19,650
2	15,900– 18,900
3	14,265– 17,085
4	11,725– 14,035
5	9,695– 11,615
6	8,090– 9,680
7	6,810– 8,160
8	5,975– 6,965

Officers whose performances have been satisfactory may also receive in-class salary increases without necessarily receiving a promotion in grade level.

Extra Benefits

In addition to base pay and salary increases, you might also consider the extra financial benefits of an overseas job for the government.

If government housing is available, you would have free housing and utilities. If not, you would receive a quarters allowance, which varies from post to post but is usually sufficient to cover all or most of housing costs.

The government would also pay your travel expenses from your home to your post and back, provided you completed your tour of duty.

You might also qualify for a post differential of from 10 to 25 per cent of your base salary if you were living under adverse conditions. The government assumes that a certain amount of hardship will be expected as part of an overseas job. However, such factors as extremely hot or cold climate, wholly inadequate housing, or strongly anti-American sentiment among the local population might be regarded as sufficient hardship to warrant a post differential. You might also receive a post allowance if the cost of living were substantially higher than in Washington, D.C.

Other points to be considered are the fringe benefits of annual leave, sick and home leave, and retirement and medical benefits, although these are usually part of employment by most big firms anywhere.

Pay for Employees of American Firms

Your best opportunity for making money abroad lies in working for an American firm. In addition to a pay scale that is usually 25 per cent higher than at home, American firms compensate employees in other ways.

For example, an overseas premium is paid to managerial employees abroad. Companies consider it an incentive to get qualified personnel overseas, and remuneration for the added hours and responsibilities common to many overseas posts.

The allowance most generally considered a real bonus is the quarters allowance, which covers all or most housing expenses and thus adds a substantial amount to the purchasing value of your paycheck.

If a company does not maintain its own quarters, as do many large oil companies, you might be allotted funds for temporary lodging until you found a permanent residence.

In some countries living costs are higher than in the United States. For instance, eggs in the Middle or Far East run as high as $4 a dozen, and a carton of cigarettes nearly that high. In such cases you would receive a post allowance to equalize costs.

If secondary education were not readily available, you might be given an education allowance to make it possible for your children to attend a private school abroad or to live with relatives and attend high school in the United States. Some companies provide round-trip transportation for college-bound young people.

In instances in which it is not possible for a man's family to accompany him to an overseas post, he is allotted a separation allowance to maintain his wife and family at home.

Other unusual allowances are offered by some companies, particularly for managers abroad, which might include language training, entertainment, automobile, and medical expenses, and club memberships.

Generally these multipayment plans take the form of overseas premiums and cost-of-living allowances or a combination of the two incentives.

Recently the Machinery and Allied Products Institute conducted a survey of companies who have personnel stationed abroad, covering most of the areas of compensation. The following are some of the findings:

1. Salaries paid to American employees abroad equal or exceed those paid employees in the United States. Two thirds of the companies surveyed also pay a premium for overseas service, with a trend toward varying premium payments according to location.

2. More than 70 per cent of the companies pay education allowances for children of American employees abroad, with the bulk of the expenditures going for the education of those below the college level.

3. Most companies reimburse overseas employees for entertainment expenses; more than half do so *only* for employees abroad.

4. About half of the companies reimburse overseas employees who are adversely affected in their tax situation because of working overseas (see Chapter VII).

5. Nearly all of the companies pay a cost-of-living allowance, with more than half using the U.S. State Department cost-of-living index as a basis for computing it.

6. Almost all companies pay at least part of the cost of shipping household goods overseas, and many also pay for adapting appliances to local use. Nearly all companies pay costs of storage and initial living expenses.

7. One third of the companies pay for first-class air travel for their employees; the remainder pay second-class fares.

8. Most companies pay for language training for their employees, and more than half will include the employee's wife and, in some cases, his family.

One executive, when explaining his company's policy of paying extra salary for overseas personnel, said, "Sure, the guy lives a lot better than the local people. But he wants to live as well as he would at home. Our philosophy is that we're asking a man to represent us in a market. And for that we offer him a premium plus cost-of-living differential so that it will be attractive for him to resettle his family in this new area. Depending on the area, it may be essential that we provide housing or facilities so he doesn't endanger his health or children's education. Certain conditions may require prestige items such as a car, an entertainment allowance, or club privileges."

Pay for Employees of Foreign Firms Abroad

If you have read this far and still think you might like to work for a foreign firm abroad, you must be prepared to accept and get along on a lower salary.

Again, it is impossible to be specific because of the many variables involved, not the least of which is the country in which you would be working.

In most countries, you would be paid according to the local scale. In some countries the minimum wages are determined through industry-wide agreements. Even then, however, the scale varies according to the degree of skill, the region of the country, and the availability of manpower.

In Belgium the average minimum wage for unskilled labor is 46 cents an hour. This brings an annual salary of not quite $1,200. Of course, the minimum wage for skilled labor is higher. The average gross wage in textiles is nearly twice as much and in shipbuilding almost three times as much.

Should you wish to work in Japan, unless you are in a very special field or have a very special skill, you cannot compete with the Japanese on the wage level. An American businessman living in Tokyo explains the situation:

"It costs a Japanese much, much less to live in a way that is comfortable to him than it would cost a foreigner. A Japanese girl who masters another language and goes into secretarial work can earn about $300 to $350 per month—considered excellent pay and pretty nearly top pay until you get into the higher levels. The average Japanese copy typist earns about $100 per month. For a foreign girl to try to get a typist's job in Japan would be ridiculous. Even if she had other office skills, she would not know the language and therefore would not be more valuable than the Japanese girl who has two languages.

"Living for a foreigner in Japan—trying to maintain any kind of Western comforts—can be very expensive. A tiny apartment, one considered second class in the United States, can easily run $100 a month and up. Living strictly Japanese style can be fun for a tourist or for a few months to the uninitiated, but, unless you are aware of what it means and have become accustomed to the style, it can be quite a transition to make."

In Turkey, minimum wages for different jobs at different locations are determined by the local committee of the Ministry of Labor.

The basic weekly wage in Australia, guaranteed by the Federal Tribunal, varies from city to city, ranging from the Australian equivalent of $32 in Sydney to $29 in Brisbane. As a general guide, unskilled and semiskilled men may expect a starting salary of $36 to $42, and recognized tradesmen, $42 to $54, for a 40-hour week. A good secretary might make $45 a week. College graduates entering industry and commerce usually begin at around $2,900 a year, and established professional men make a minimum annual salary of $5,700.

These figures are based on the current exchange rate of one Australian pound to $2.24. While the pay rates seem low, they are generally sufficient to support the employees at a standard of living very little below that of the United States.

It might be well to remember, however, that if you intend to return some of your pay to the United States, the money you make in Australia would not buy as much at home. This is also true of Great Britain, where wages are lower than in the United States and the cost of living is generally lower.

In South Africa, where prices are just about half of what they are here, wages are quite high. A clerk, secretary, or accountant might earn as much as $350 a month, which would give him purchasing power of nearly $700.

CHAPTER VII

U.S. Taxes on Salary Earned Abroad

You will not be taxed by the United States government on income earned abroad if:

1. You are not an employee of the government.
2. You establish a bona fide foreign residence or meet physical-presence requirements in a foreign country.
3. All of your earned income is made in a foreign country.
4. Your income does not exceed $20,000.

Perhaps we should expand on these requirements, since some of them are rather complex.

1. As a civilian employee of the government abroad, you would have much the same tax situation as a member of the armed forces. All of your income would be taxable, including post differentials for stations outside the United States and in Alaska and Hawaii. Cost-of-living and foreign-area allowances are excludable.

2. If you work in a foreign country for private industry or are self-employed, your tax-exempt income could prove to be quite considerable; but to qualify for this exemption you must meet the all-important requirements of bona fide foreign residence or physical presence.

In order to qualify for exemption under the bona fide residence requirement you must, obviously, establish a foreign residence. However, this bona fide residence is not necessarily your domicile. Your domicile is your fixed and permanent abode, to which you always return or intend to return. You might have your domicile in Milwaukee, for example, and still have a bona fide residence in Rome if you went there to work and established yourself in the community. You would have created an "air of stability" about your stay in Rome, even if you intended ultimately to return to Milwaukee.

Of course, there are many borderline cases, and each must be evaluated individually. The authorities would use such deciding factors as the purpose of your trip and the length of your stay abroad. It can be said, however, that in order to establish bona fide residence you must not make a statement to the authorities of the country involved that you are not a resident, and you must be considered sufficiently a resident to make you subject to the income tax of that country if one exists.

Bona fide residence must include an entire tax year, that is, from January 1 to December 31. Though this is generally construed to mean an uninterrupted stay, you may leave the country for short trips to the United States or elsewhere, whether for business or for vacation, provided you have a clear intention to return to your foreign residence or to a new foreign residence "without undue delay."

Merely living in another country for a year does not necessarily exempt you from United States income tax, however. A worker on a construction project, for example, would remain only until the job was completed. He would not go overseas with a clear intention to establish a bona fide residence.

The requirements of physical presence are more clearly defined. You are exempt from paying U.S. income tax under the physical-presence requirement if:

a. You are in a foreign country, or countries, for at least 510 days (roughly 17 months) in any consecutive 18-month period.
b. You are not paid by the United States government or one of its agencies.
c. Your earned income is for personal services rendered outside the United States.

The physical-presence test is not concerned with the nature of your stay, your intentions of returning, or the kind of residence you establish. It is concerned only with the duration of your stay.

In a sense, this test gives you 18 consecutive months in which to acquire the 510 days, and you need only be on foreign soil to qualify. It is unconditional, however. If you were forced to return home because of illness or any other reason, you would not meet the requirements and would have to pay tax.

Although you may travel from country to country and still qualify for the exemption, you would lose qualifying days for any 24-hour period in which you were traveling on or over international waters.

3. Once you have established your foreign residence or met the physical-presence test, you must be able to show that your earned income was made in a foreign country.

Only earned income is tax-exempt; unearned income is not. Earned income is acquired through salaries, wages, commissions, or professional fees. Unearned income includes income from business in which you have no part except investment, dividends, interest, some royalties, alimony, and gambling gains. In that gray area between earned and unearned, between taxable and untaxable, are the variables of pensions, annuities, and rents for property that you own but do not maintain.

The Internal Revenue Service says you must be paid by "sources outside the United States." This refers to the place where you work, not to the place from which your wages or salary are paid. Thus you could earn your income in Italy, say, even if your paycheck came from the New York office of your company. It would make no difference if you received your earnings at your foreign address or had them deposited in an American bank.

4. If you qualify under either the residence or physical-presence requirements, your income is tax-exempt up to $20,000 a year, or $35,000 a year if you have stayed abroad for three consecutive years.

If, however, you left before a full tax year was up, you would be required to prorate your tax exemption to the number of qualifying days you spent abroad.

Several other items must be mentioned.

First, even if your income is all tax-exempt, you must file an income-tax return.

Second, income must be reported in United States dollars. This would create a problem only for, say, a government employee who received all or part of his income in foreign currency.

Third, you may deduct any foreign income or other taxes imposed on you. These must be bona fide taxes and do not include title fees, tolls, water bills, marriage licenses, or dog licenses.

Foreign Income Taxes

Foreign governments not only can, but probably will, tax your income if you establish residence and work in the country for any length of time. Since taxes vary widely from country to country, it is difficult, if not impossible, to estimate them.

The United States is a party to a number of tax treaties limiting in varying ways the taxes that signatories may impose on noncitizens. Because these treaties are complex and vary from country to country, it may be well to discuss one of them briefly, to give you an idea of how they would affect you as an alien.

Denmark has a double taxation convention with the United States providing that wages and salaries you earn as a resident of Denmark are not subject to Danish taxation if:

1. You maintain your U.S. residence.
2. You do not earn more than $3,000.
3. You do not stay in Denmark more than 90 days—or 180 days if you are working for an American business during any tax year.

If, however, you were subject to Danish taxation, the U.S. government would give you credit for those taxes, and you would be subject to U.S. taxation only on the balance.

When you take up residence in Denmark, you become liable to payment of income tax as of January 1, April 1, July 1, or October 1, whichever dates follows your arrival in Denmark.

Although personal income tax in Denmark is fixed each year by legislation, the rates are generally higher for low- and middle-income brackets and lower for high-income brackets than in the United States.

On the subject of taxes, we might add that United States Social Security taxes apply to overseas employment. If you expect to collect Social Security benefits on retirement, you must continue to contribute while you are employed overseas by an American firm or by the U.S. government. If, however, you work for a foreign firm, the Social Security Administration would determine your benefits according to the contributions you had made.

This is just a general outline of the factors that enter in the tax considerations of your job abroad. For more information, ask for a booklet entitled "Tax Guide for U.S. Citizens Abroad" at your nearest Internal Revenue office. Or you may write to:

U.S. Treasury Department
Internal Revenue Service
Washington, D.C.

CHAPTER VIII

Getting the Job

There's nothing to it! Arrive as a tourist (you'd better have funds for the return home or you may not be allowed to enter), find a job, have your employer get you a work permit, and in a very real sense "you're in business."

It all sounds easy, and perhaps—just perhaps—it might go that smoothly. But how do you take that second step—"find a job"?

Where Do You Look?

First, you might go to the American Embassy. Although finding jobs for Americans is hardly their *raison d'être,* they might have some leads, and someone might even know of an open position. They certainly could give you the names of American companies doing business in that country, although American companies seldom hire directly for overseas posts, usually sending someone from within the company.

However, armed with such a list, you could make the rounds of personnel offices. This could be a long procedure, and you would be well advised to have enough money to wait it out.

If you are fortunate, perhaps you have friends who have friends who might know of a job for you. But don't pester them. Let them know you are looking and what you can do, and then go off on your own to try other channels.

The newspaper help-wanted columns are a useful source. In England the London *Times* and *Daily Telegraph* and the Manchester *Guardian* take ads from prospective employers and from job seekers. Trade and professional publications also carry notices of employment opportunities and can be consulted in some of the many libraries in the United Kingdom. One word of warning: Although most firms or individuals advertising for employees are sincere, an affidavit of good character is not required by most newspapers accepting advertising, so be alert.

If an American military post is nearby, you might inquire about openings for civilian employees. You might be fortunate enough to get a job by being there at the right time.

Unless you have unlimited funds, however, it is certainly not advisable to go overseas in the hope of getting a job by "being in the right place at the right time." We might reiterate the question of the U.S. Chamber of Commerce quoted in the first chapter:

"Can you risk being stranded, penniless, on foreign shores after attempts to find a job have failed?"

Obviously, jobs are hardest to find in the largest cities—Paris, Rome, and London. But you might consider cutting rice in the south of France at $50 a month plus room and board, or picking grapes in the vineyard region from August to October, and seeing parts of France of which many Paris residents are not even aware.

Getting a Job in Advance

A good first step in getting a job before leaving home is to consult foreign newspapers before you leave this country. In addition to jobs advertised in the classified section, a newspaper by its very nature is full of information about what is being thought and done in its city and country of publication. And a corollary advantage is the chance to brush up on your foreign-language reading skills.

If newspapers of the country of your interest are not at a library, write to the embassy or information center and ask their help in securing copies.

Field offices of the U.S. Department of Commerce (see the Appendix for the addresses) can provide a listing by country of American firms that operate abroad; these lists are available for a dollar each.

When you have a listing of the firms that operate in the country in which you are interested, you can get information about the individual companies and the name and address of the personnel manager from one of the following directories, most of which are available at public libraries.

American Register of Exporters and Importers. American Register of Exporters, New York.

Poor's Register of Directors and Executives, Standard and Poor's Corp., New York.

Thomas Register of Manufacturers. Thomas Publishing Company, New York.

National and International Employment Handbook for Specialized Personnel, J. L. Angel, World Trade Academy Press, New York.

Angel's National Directory of Personnel Managers, J. L. Angel World Trade Academy Press, New York.

Dun and Bradstreet Reference Directory, Dun and Bradstreet, New York.

Since many of the firms employing help overseas have New York offices, the New York newspapers are generally the best source of job information, particularly the listings of employment agencies that specialize in overseas work. These are probably your best bet for finding work with an American firm.

In many ways an employment agency is like a real estate agency. If you wanted to sell your house and didn't want to take the time and trouble of selling it yourself, you would list it with a real estate agent.

Employment agencies work in the same way. They have listings ranging from top managerial positions to jobs requiring skilled manual labor. Since they often know the personal quirks of prospective employers, they usually require a personal visit in order to determine whether you have the personality as well as the skill and experience required.

Usually these agencies are licensed and bonded by the state in which they operate. Of course, you must be prepared to pay for their services, just as you would pay a real estate agent.

One agency reports that its fee is 60 per cent of the first month's foreign salary at the job site for jobs that pay over $400 a month, and only rarely does the agency handle lower-paid jobs. To justify the size of the fee, the agency tells of two men placed despite lack of mechanical, technical, or professional skills or overseas experience. They earned $8,000 to $9,000 a year, plus all expenses (travel, food, quarters, and medical), on an 18-month contract. This made their income tax-exempt in the United States, and the foreign country assessed no income tax. Thus they were able to save $12,000 to $13,000 in their 18 months of foreign service. A $9,000 annual salary equals a monthly salary of $750, and the 60 per cent agency fee amounted to $450. This was their investment to realize rather considerable earning power.

Embassies and American Chambers of Commerce

American Chambers of Commerce are in operation in 21 foreign countries, and most of them are affiliated with the United States Chamber of Commerce. Some have a clearing-house service for job opportunities and often include information of this kind in the periodicals they publish.

These periodicals also carry feature articles on life and activities in the country and could be very helpful to anyone planning to spend some time abroad.

For a complete listing of the foreign offices of American Chambers of Commerce abroad, plus general information on their activities, send 25 cents to:

Foreign Commerce-Foreign Policy Department
Chamber of Commerce of the United States
Washington, D.C. 20006

Some embassies and consulates can also provide job leads.
The *Australian Consulate General* suggests addressing inquiries directly to:

The Secretary
Department of Labour and National Service
Post Office Box 2817AA
Melbourne, C.I., Victoria, Australia

Include in your letter your full name, date of birth, and details of education, vocational training, and employment experience. If you have a preference as to where you would like to work in Australia, it would be wise to include that as well as the type of work you would like to do. If you are married, include the number and ages of your children.

Australian employers, like employers everywhere, usually prefer not to commit themselves until an interview has been held, but the National Employment Service can provide you with up-to-date information.

The *Austrian Embassy* advises that, to obtain information on the job situation in that country, you address your inquiry to:

Bundesministerium für Soziale Verwaltung
Wien I, Regierungsgebäude

If you would like to work in *Bermuda,* the Trade Development Board suggests advertising in one of the local newspapers—the *Bermuda Sun,* the *Mid-Ocean News* or the *Royal Gazette,* all in Hamilton, the capital.

If you would like hotel work, write directly to the managers of the larger hotels. Most hotels employ Bermudians as waitresses, but exceptions are made.

The major hotels are:

Belmont Golf and Country Club, Warwick Parish
Bermudian Hotel, Pembroke Parish
Carlton Beach Hotel, Southampton Parish
Castle Harbour Hotel, Hamilton Parish
Elbow Beach Surf Club, Paget Parish
Inverurie Hotel, Paget Parish
Princess Hotel, Pembroke Parish
St. George Hotel, St. George

The *Embassy of Costa Rica* suggests writing to the Ministry of Labor and Social Welfare for information about work opportunities. In addition, private groups deal with specialized fields:

Camara de Industrias (Industry)
Camara de Agricultura (Agriculture)
Camara de Ganaderia (Cattle)
Camara de Comercio (Merchants)
Asoc. Nal. de Educadores (Education)
Junta de Proteccion Social

The *Danish Embassy* will provide you with a list of newspapers in which you might advertise for work in Denmark. The leading newspapers and their addresses are:

Berlingske Tidende, Pilestraede 34, Copenhagen K, Denmark
Politiken, Radhuspladsen, Copenhagen V, Denmark
Aktuelt, Norre Farimagsgade 43, Copenhagen K, Denmark

For information on jobs in *Germany,* write to Lufthansa Airlines'
New York office for a copy of a brochure designed to help Americans
locate jobs in the Federal Republic.
You may also write directly to:

Zentralstelle für Arbeitsvermittlung
6 Frankfort-am-Main
Eschersheimer Landstrasse 1–7

The reply will bring you more detailed information on opportunities
for work in Germany. Two application forms will be enclosed for
you to fill out (in German) and return to the agency. With luck, this
correspondence will be followed by a letter from the placement agency
telling you the name of your new employer and the terms of your
work. Since both of these letters are form letters, you might assume
correctly that not only are there many inquiries about work in Germany, but there are many placements of aliens in jobs.
The *Consulate of Israel* will tell you that information on job openings can be obtained from the:

Committee on Manpower Opportunities in Israel
515 Park Avenue
New York 22, N.Y.

If you are confident enough of your language skills to work in
Japan, you might try an advertisement in the *Japan Times,* Tokyo,
the English-language newspaper. The American Chamber of Commerce in Japan warns that the help-wanted ads specifying "English
required" usually mean Japanese who can speak English.
The *Mexican Embassy* will provide you with a list of employment
agencies in Mexico City, with no recommendation except that they
are listed as such in the telephone book.

Agencia Palma, Ave. Chapultepec 108-D, Mexico, D.F.
Sr. Lorenzo Mondragon, Ave. Chapultepec 32-2, Mexico, D.F.

Harry Wright, Xola 525, Mexico, D.F.

Sr. Samuel Bolling Wright, Xola 525, Mexico, D.F. (a separate listing from Harry Wright, but at the same address)

David Sanchez y Sota, Londres 56, Mexico, D.F.

Ana Sofia Villanueva, Campeche 433-C, Mexico, D.F.

Another source of job information in Mexico might be the weekly personnel bulletin published by the American Chamber of Commerce in Mexico, Lucerna 78, Mexico 6, D.F. If you will send a picture of yourself, a résumé, and a check for $2, the organization will publish your query.

The *Royal Netherlands Embassy* offers its help in getting a job. You might contact the United States Embassy at The Hague or the United States Consulate General at either Amsterdam or Rotterdam.

Anyone interested in working for the Panama Canal Company in the *Canal Zone* should send a completed copy of Standard Form 57, available at your local Post Office to:

Central Employment Office
Box 2008
Balboa Heights, Canal Zone.

This office maintains an applicant's supply file and Civil Service registers for all federal agencies in the Canal Zone.

In Conclusion

This has been a rather general chapter on how you might begin to look for work overseas. For obvious reasons, we have not mentioned self-employed persons or those who wish to set up businesses abroad.

We shall talk in Chapter XI about government jobs and how to get them. We shall also talk later about what Manpower, Inc., can do for you.

In the next chapter we shall deal more specifically with how to apply to an American company for a job abroad.

CHAPTER IX

How to Apply to American Companies for a Job Abroad

We have suggested generally some of the aspects of working for American private industry abroad, but let us take a minute to restate some of them:

1. Working for an American firm abroad generally makes it possible for you to earn more than if you worked for the government or for a foreign firm.
2. An American employer usually arranges for your travel, housing, and medical expenses.
3. An American employer generally secures the necessary work and residence permits and helps you in the intricacies of American and foreign taxes.
4. Most American firms' employees abroad are *not* Americans.
5. American firms normally do not hire Americans directly for overseas work, but prefer to give overseas training to someone already familiar with company operations.

It is primarily this last point that we shall discuss in this chapter. Of course, there are exceptions. Firms sometimes do hire an employee specifically for an overseas branch or subsidiary, but it is not generally done. A company has a great deal at stake in setting up an overseas branch or subsidiary. It may be competing with local firms for business, or it may be there under government contract. In either case, the good will of the host nation is vital, as is the good will of the people most directly affected by the company.

It is expensive for an American firm to send an employee abroad. It must send not only the most reliable person, but also one intimately acquainted with company operations. For this reason, salaries are designed to attract the best people for overseas work, but requirements are equally high. Clearly, then, such jobs are not easy to get. If you want to work abroad for American industry, you can, but you will have to work at it.

As far as skills are concerned, the field is wide open. Almost every segment of the American economy touches the foreign field in one way or another, and this will be increasingly true as the years pass. But some branches of business are more actively engaged than others in overseas work. These include mining and oil companies, manufacturers, construction firms, transportation companies and travel agencies, advertising agencies, and some publishers.

How might you plan your campaign to get a job with one of these firms? Here is a brief outline that may help you:

1. Get a list of the companies operating in the country or countries in which you would like to work.
2. Select those that might need your skills.
3. Write a letter of application requesting an interview.
4. Prepare a good résumé.
5. At an interview, be prepared to sell yourself and show your prospective employer that you really want the job and can be an asset to his business.

Let us take these points one at a time:

1. *Get a list of companies operating abroad.*

A partial list of such companies is given in Chapter X. If you really want a job abroad, however, you must make your own list, which involves considerable time and study. Be sure, also, to investigate the reliability of the companies to which you apply.

We have suggested some sources for leads. In addition to the companies listed in this book, it would be wise to consult the lists available at the field offices of the U.S. Department of Commerce, located in many major cities (see the Appendix).

Check the newspapers, particularly New York newspapers, for help-wanted ads and for leads in the news columns of new or expanding businesses abroad.

If you have $75 to invest, you might subscribe to the "Foreign Projects Newsletter," published biweekly by the R-L Press, 945 Venice Boulevard, Los Angeles, California. It carries lists of economic expansion plans and programs, American firms in international operations, and contract awards. Its sources are official publications of national governments and international agencies.

Consult your library for trade publications in your field and other foreign-trade listings.

2. *Select a company that might need your skills.*

It is pointless to send out a flood of letters to companies that have no place for you. Concentrate your efforts on companies engaged in fields in which you have training or experience and in which you can make a contribution.

This will take research, and the directories listed in Chapter VIII might be a starting point. Find out as much as possible about a company and its operations before you apply.

3. *Write a letter of application.*

The main purpose of your first letter to a prospective employer is to request an interview. Only if you can interest the employer or the personnel manager in what you can do for him will he invite you to come to see him. You will be competing with many other applicants, and your letter must stand out from the rest. It should be an irresistible invitation to the employer to read it from beginning to end; it should leave him no alternative but to make an appointment with you.

How can you achieve this? Here are some ground rules:

a. Write in your own style, freely and naturally. Never copy a letter designed by someone else; it won't sound like you. Take plenty of time and give plenty of thought to the preparation of your letter.

b. Include all the information that the employer will want to have before granting an interview:

Your full name and age.
Your address and telephone number.
Your most recent school experience.
Your marital status.
Personality traits, such as hobbies and skills.
Your hopes for the future in a working career.
Your experience that ties in with the job you are seeking.

Omit any reference to the salary you expect; time enough to talk about that if you get the interview.

c. Remember that businessmen are busy and will not read all the way through a long letter. Make yours short and to the point.

d. Give the gist of your story in the opening paragraph. This is an axiom in advertising and newspaper reporting—to insure reader interest, begin with the core of what you have to say.

e. Don't be satisfied with the first draft. Read over every word several times. Strike out all unnecessary words, phrases, and sentences. Keep reminding yourself that you are trying to obtain an interview, not land a job. First things first—your letter should be a door opener for you; it should include only essential and pertinent information.

f. Be sure the letter is neat and attractive in appearance. If possible, type it or have it typed. A sloppy letter seriously hampers your chances.

g. Enclose a good current photograph. Avoid old ones, posed studio photographs, and vacation snapshots.

h. Type each letter individually. Never send carbon copys. If you plan to send out a number of letters, it will be worth the money to have them prepared by a firm specializing in autotyped or Hooven letters that look like originals. Time the mailing of your letter so that it will not arrive on a Monday or a Friday, usually the employers' busiest days.

i. Before you seal the envelope and drop it in the mailbox, check over for the last time the following points in your letter:

Is it properly addressed?
Is it neat?
Are the spelling, grammar, and punctuation correct?
Does the opening paragraph tell the story?
Is it concise and to the point?
Is it from the employer's point of view?
Is it courteous?
Is the material presented in orderly, logical fashion?
Has it the ring of sincerity?

One college graduate, after surveying employment prospects, sent out 178 individually typed letters to firms doing business abroad. In each letter he requested an interview and enclosed a résumé and a photograph. He received 135 replies (six were form letters), but only 12 offered interviews.

The sequel to this story of a determined young man was that he accepted employment as a sales trainee with a possibility, although not a promise, of working overseas.

4. *Prepare a good résumé.*

If you are looking for work in a professional or specialized field, it is always helpful to prepare a résumé. This is a written catalog of what you have to offer an employer.

The résumé should state briefly your work experience, your training and education, personal facts, and the type of work you are seeking. Prepare it carefully—it is your plan of attack as you begin a campaign for a job. It must "sell" you to the prospective employer.

Be concise, stick to the facts. Remember, the employer is interested in finding out all he can about your qualifications in as short a time as possible. Present the facts in a down-to-earth, straightforward fashion, in the terse style you might use in a telegram. A résumé is no place for literary flourishes. It is, in effect, a handy map or chart of yourself in terms of your professional or technical life.

Here is an example of the kind of information you might include:

Name
Address
Telephone number
Personal data:
   Age, height, and weight
   Marital status
   Number and ages of children

Education:
   Include any special training for the job you seek, and honors and awards if pertinent. College graduates should list pertinent courses, including languages.

Experience:
   Begin with the most recent job and work back. If any job included supervisory experience, be sure to mention it. Include, too, a brief statement of duties that might apply to the job you are seeking.

Professional or Technical Associations

Military Service

Hobbies

Some people choose to include two additional items: objective, and references. Opinion is divided on the value of a statement of objective. Those who favor it hold that an employer likes to have some idea of an applicant's goal. Those who oppose it feel that it must be either so general that it says nothing, or so specific that it narrows the field in which you might potentially be employed. The choice is up to you.

References, if you choose to give them, might include professional contacts and former employers. In applying for overseas work, it may be wise to include character references, since the employer will be interested not only in your ability in the job, but also in your ability to represent the company effectively.

Some employers are suspicious of references, believing that you would mention only people who would give you a boost. For this reason, you might merely state that you will furnish references upon request.

5. *The interview.*

Much has been written on how to put your best foot forward at an interview. Although there are no hard and fast rules, certain points should be borne in mind.

Dress neatly, conservatively, and in good taste. This will show the interviewer that you care about your appearance and will boost your own spirits. For a woman, a hat and gloves are necessary. For a man, a business suit makes a better impression than a sport jacket and slacks.

Be on time. Plan to arrive five or ten minutes early so that you can collect your thoughts before your interview.

Answer questions honestly. If you don't know, say so. If some of the questions seem personal, understand that the interviewer is not prying, but only trying to find out what kind of person you are.

Be prepared for questions that seem to have little bearing on you as a future employee. You might be asked:

Why do you want to work for this company?

Why would you like to go overseas? Or to a particular country?

What books do you read in your spare time? (He doesn't want a plot outline of the last novel you read, just a list of some of the books you have read as an indication of your interests.)

What do you think are your biggest weaknesses?

A future employer has a right to know why you left or are leaving your last job. If the reason falls in the area of a personality clash, be sure to take part of the blame yourself. Don't run down your last employer.

Sometimes questions are asked not so much for the answer as for your readiness to answer or as a test of your thinking ability.

Most interviewers will give you an opportunity to ask questions, and this is your cue to show your interest in the company and your knowledge of it. Ask specific questions that you have not been able to answer in your research. Plan your questions and ask them intelligently.

Finally, if you are offered a job overseas, weigh the terms of employment carefully. You will doubtless be asked to sign a contract; read it carefully, since a broken contract can mean financial problems as well as legal ones.

A contract will include such matters as a definition of the work you are to do, the location of your work, salary, reassignment, length of service for which the contract is binding, living allowance, travel expenses to and from the job, business expenses, and the terms under which the contract will end.

As I said at the beginning, although some companies hire people specifically for overseas work, most do not. Usually the employees sent abroad are those with long experience in the firm who are ready to assume the additional responsibilities of overseas work. A job-seeker who wants to go abroad should first be interested in the company itself, although he certainly should let his employer know of his ultimate interest in employment abroad. He should take any suitable job with a company having foreign interests, and then work toward his long-range objective.

CHAPTER X

American Companies That Operate Abroad

In the last chapter we discussed how you might compile a list of prospective employers who have operations abroad. In this one we shall give a partial list as a starter for you.

It is impossible to provide a complete list, because conditions change from day to day. Generally, however, the change will be toward more companies rather than fewer. The current trend is toward expanding operations and entry of more companies into the field.

Some of the companies listed have only financial interests in the country mentioned and may not have any employees there. If they do indeed employ abroad, it must be understood that the majority of their employees are probably nationals. The ratio is often as high as one hundred nationals to one American employed by a single company.

The reason for this is simple. An American company operating abroad receives tax benefits as well as a ready market for its products. In return, it supports the local economy by providing jobs.

The following companies, listed in alphabetical order, employ Americans for their overseas operations.

Acco International, 280 Madison Avenue, New York, New York. Office and school supplies and equipment in Australia, England, Mexico, and countries of the European Economic Community.

Airtool Manufacturing Company, 302 South Center Street, Springfield, Ohio 45501. Manufacturers of pneumatic hand tools, tube cleaners and expanders. Employs machinists and sales personnel in Europe.

Eaton Yale and Towne, Inc., 405 Lexington Avenue, New York 10017. Manufacturers and distributors of Yale locks and hardware in Mexico, Colombia, Philippines, Japan.

Joseph T. Ryerson and Son, Inc., P. O. Box 8000A, Chicago, Illinois.
Distribution and processing of steel, aluminum, plastics, and metal-working machinery in The Netherlands.

Sta-Rite Products, Inc., Delavan, Wisconsin.
Manufacturers of pumps and water systems for farm, home, and industry in Canada.

Steiner Company, 740 Rush Street, Chicago, Illinois 60611.
Contracts the manufacture of cloth and paper towel cabinets and sells from its Swiss offices. Sales personnel and management trainees in Europe, South America, Australia, South Africa, Japan.

Toledo Scale Corporation, Telegraph Road, Toledo, Ohio. Manufacture, sale, and service of commercial and industrial weighing and food-processing equipment. Employs engineering and technical personnel in Brazil, Mexico, Belgium, Germany.

United Carbon Division (Ashland Oil and Refining Company), Box 1502, Houston, Texas.
Manufactures and sells carbon black. Interested in applicants for positions as general manager, controller, sales manager, technical sales and plant manager in Australia, France, England, Venezuela, India.

World Trade Academy Press, Inc., 50 East 42nd Street, New York, N.Y. 10017.
Publishes in the field of international marketing. Interested in applicants in overseas management and international public relations and marketing in Colombia, Venezuela, Argentina, Spain, Japan.

Worthington Corp., Worthington Avenue, Harrison, N.J. 07029.
Manufacture and sale of pumps, compressors, turbines, engines, valves, air-conditioning and electrical equipment. Positions for young graduate engineers leading to overseas assignments as sales engineers and area managers in Latin America, Southeast Asia, Far East, Near East, Africa.

Wurlitzer Company, DeKalb, Illinois 60115.
Manufacture and sale of pianos, organs, coin-operated phonographs. Interested in multilingual sales and service personnel in England, Switzerland, Germany.

Wyeth International, Ltd., Box 8299, Philadelphia, Pa. 19101.
Pharmaceutical manufacturers. International sales and sales promotion executives worldwide.

Many of the above companies require a training period in this country before sending employees abroad. The situation in which many companies find themselves is well stated by O. V. Peterson, manager of international operations for the Aluminum Company of America.

"Since our operations require specific technical operating and engineering know-how, or marketing techniques, our facilities are staffed with personnel from our domestic system who have had considerable experience in the aluminum field. With a nucleus of trained Alcoans to start with, competent local personnel are hired and trained in the various phases of our business, both technical and marketing. This training may be accomplished on the site or, in some instances, in our U.S. facilities. After local nationals have achieved the necessary skills and experience, they are upgraded to fill positions which originally were held by American expatriates."

Deere and Company says: "Individuals sent over from the United States are in many cases specialists or top management personnel."

Rheem Manufacturing Company says "All of our foreign operations are staffed by nationals of the host country."

Sears Roebuck and Company writes: "Our international operation rarely, if ever, sends executives overseas who are not Sears-trained personnel. In this regard, we do not consider a person qualified until he has established at least five years or more service domestically."

Socony Mobil Oil Company, Inc., says: "Generally speaking, we do not recruit directly for overseas positions. We recruit young persons for careers in Socony Mobil operations wherever in the world they might be. As a rule, employees must prove themselves in domestic employment before being assigned to overseas positions."

Of course, hundreds of other companies have operations overseas, and we shall list some of them, by country.

The companies with the largest operations abroad are often those that are the largest in this country—General Motors, Standard Oil of New Jersey, Ford Motor Company, Chrysler Corporation, Monsanto, and Coca-Cola, to mention just a few.

While the following list does not pretend to be complete, it is a place to start. We cannot assure you, however, that the firms have any openings for overseas personnel, much less an opening for you. It might also be noted that the list omits firms with obvious worldwide operations, such as airlines, shipping firms, hotels, and communications or news agencies.

AUSTRALIA

Abbott Laboratories International

American Can Co.

American Cyanamid Co.

American Smelting & Refining Co.

American Steel Foundries, Inc.

Arrow Hart & Hegeman Electric Co.

Automatic Electric Co.

Black & Decker Manufacturing Co.

Borden Corp.

Borg-Warner Corp.

Bristol-Myers Co.

Bucyrus-Erie Co.

Burlington Mills Corp.

Canada Dry International, Inc.

Carborundum Co.

Chrysler Corp.

Coca-Cola Co.

Colgate-Palmolive International, Inc.

Conde Nast Publications, Inc.

Continental Can Co., Inc.

Eastman Kodak Co.

Elizabeth Arden Corp.

Ford Motor Co.

General American Transportation Corp.

General Motors Corp.

Gillette Co.

Goodyear Tire & Rubber Co.

H. J. Heinz Co.

Ingersoll-Rand Co.

International Business Machines Corp.

International Telephone & Telegraph Corp.

Johnson & Johnson

S. C. Johnson & Son, Inc.

Joy Manufacturing Co.

Kellogg Co.

Lever Brothers Co.

Lincoln Electric Co.

Manpower Inc.

Masonite Corp.

Max Factor & Co.

Merck & Co., Inc.

Monsanto Chemical Co.

National Cash Register Co.

National Lead Co.

Orange Crush Co.

Otis Elevator Co.

Parke, Davis & Co.

Pepsi-Cola Co.

Philip Morris, Inc.

Reichhold Chemicals, Inc.
Remington Rand Corp.
St. Regis Paper Co.
Scoville Manufacturing Co.
Sherwin-Williams Co.
Singer Co., Inc.
Smith, Kline & French Laboratories
Standard Oil Co. of New Jersey
Standard Vacuum Oil Co.
Sterling Drug Co.
Stromberg-Carlson Co.
Sunbeam Corp.
Swift & Co.
Sylvania Electric Products, Inc.
Vick Chemical Co.
Westinghouse Electric Corp.
Wilson & Co., Inc.
Wm. Wrigley, Jr., Co.

AUSTRIA

American Standard Corp.
Standard Oil Co. of New Jersey

BELGIUM

Abbott Laboratories International
American Foreign Insurance Association
American Standard Corp.
Armour & Co.
Atlantic Refining Co.
Burroughs Corp.
Chrysler Corp.
Coca-Cola Export Co.
Colgate-Palmolive International Inc.
Corn Products Refining Co.
Crown Cork & Seal Corp.
Eastman Kodak Co.
Ford Motor Co.
General Motors Corp.

Guaranty Trust Co. of New York
Gulf Oil Corp.
Ingersoll-Rand Co.
International Harvester Co.
International Business Machines Corp.
International Telephone & Telegraph Corp.
Johns-Manville Corp.
Joy Manufacturing Co.
Libby, McNeill & Libby
Manpower Inc.
Minneapolis Cash Register Co.
Olin-Mathieson Chemical Corp.
Otis Elevator Co.
Parke, Davis & Co.
Pfizer International, Inc.
Pittsburgh Plate Glass Co.
Procter & Gamble Distributing Co.
Remington Rand Corp.
St. Regis Paper Co.
Singer Co., Inc.
Smith-Corona Marchant Inc.
Standard Oil Co.
Sun Oil Co.
J. Walter Thompson, Inc.
United States Rubber Co.
United States Steel Corp.

BOLIVIA

Abbott Laboratories International
American Smelting & Refining Co.
Foster Wheeler Corp.

BRAZIL

Abbott Laboratories International
Addressograph-Multigraph Corp.
Admiral Corp.

American Chicle Corp.
American Cyanamid Co.
American Foreign Insurance Association
American Home Products Corp.
American Machine & Foundry Co.
Anderson, Clayton & Co.
Armco Steel Corp.
Armour & Co.
Atlantic Refining Co.
B. T. Babbitt, Inc.
Bausch & Lomb, Inc.
Bethlehem Steel Corp.
Black & Decker Manufacturing Co.
Borden Co.
Bristol-Myers Co.
Carrier Corp.
J. I. Case Co.
Caterpillar Tractors Co., Inc.
Coca-Cola Co.
Colgate-Palmolive International, Inc.
Columbia Records Division
Corning Glass Works
Coty International Corp.
Crown Cork & Seal Corp.
E. I. du Pont de Nemours & Co.
Eastman Kodak Co.
Ebasco International Corp.
Esso-Standard Oil Co.
Falk Corp.
Firemen's Insurance Co.
Firestone Tire & Rubber Co.
First National Bank of Boston
First National City Bank
Ford Motor Co.
Fruehauf Trailer Division
Gardner-Denver Co.
General Electric Co.
General Motors Acceptance Corp.

Geophysical Services, Inc.
Gillette Co.
B. F. Goodrich Co.
Goodyear Tire & Rubber Co.
W. R. Grace Co.
Grant Advertising, Inc.
A. P. Green Fire Brick Co.
Griffith Laboratories, Inc.
Gulf Oil Corp.
Helena Rubinstein, Inc.
Hoffman-La Roche, Inc.
Home Fittings International
Home Insurance Co.
Ingersoll-Rand Co.
International Basic Economy Corp.
International Business Machines Corp.
International Electric Corp.
International Nickel Co., Inc.
International Packers, Ltd.
International Telephone & Telegraph Corp.
Johnson & Johnson
S. C. Johnson & Son, Inc.
Jones & Laughlin Steel Corp.
Kellogg Co.
Koppers Co.
Lehn & Fink Products Co.
Lentheric, Inc.
Le Tourneau-Westinghouse Co.
Eli Lilly & Co.
Liquid Carbonic Corp.
Lone Star Cement Corp.
Manpower Inc.
Martin Marietta Corp.
Max Factor & Co.
McCann Erickson, Inc.
McGraw-Hill, Inc.
Merck & Co., Inc.
Miles Laboratories, Inc.
Minnesota Mining & Manufacturing Co.

Moore-McCormack Lines, Inc.
Morrison-Knudsen Co., Inc.
National Cash Register Co.
National Lead Co.
Olin-Mathieson Chemical Corp.
Orange Crush Co.
Otis Elevator Co.
Parke Davis & Co.
Pepsi-Cola Co.
Pfizer International, Inc.
Philco International Corp.
Pittsburgh Plate Glass Co.
Quaker Oats International Co.
Raybest Manhattan, Inc.
Reichhold Chemicals, Inc.
Republic Chemical Corp.
Republic Pictures International
 Co.
Revere Copper & Brass, Inc.
RKO Radio Pictures Division
St. Regis Paper Co.
Seven-Up Export Corp.
Sherwin-Williams Co.
Singer Co., Inc.
Smith-Corona Marchant, Inc.
Sperry Rand Corp.
E. R. Squibb & Sons Division
Standard Brands, Inc.
Standard Oil Co. of California
Standard Oil Co. of New Jersey
Sterling Drug, Inc.
Swift & Co.
Taylor Instrument Companies
Texaco, Inc.
J. Walter Thompson Co.
Thor Power Tool Co.
Union Carbide Corp.
United Shoe Machinery Corp.
United States Rubber Co.
United States Steel Corp.
Universal International Films,
 Inc.
Universal Match Corp.

Warner-Lambert Pharmaceutical
 Co.

CHILE

Abbott Laboratories Interna-
 tional
Anaconda Co.
Bethlehem Steel Corp.
E. I. du Pont de Nemours & Co.
First National City Bank
Ford Motor Co.
General Motors Corp.
W. R. Grace & Co.
International Business Machines
 Corp.
Kennecott Copper Corp.
Manpower Inc.
Phelps Dodge Corp.
Singer Co., Inc.
Standard Oil Co. of New Jersey
United Shoe Machinery Corp.
United States Rubber Co.

COLOMBIA

Abbott Laboratories Inter-
 national
American Chicle Co.
American Coffee Corp.
American Foreign Insurance
 Association
Armco Steel Corp.
Borden Co.
Burlington International
Burroughs Corp.
Caterpillar Tractors Co., Inc.
Celanese Corp. of America
Cities Service Oil Co.
Cluett Peabody & Co., Inc.
Coca-Cola Co.
Colgate-Palmolive International,
 Inc.
Container Corp. of America
Continental Can Co.

Corn Products Refining Co.
Dun and Bradstreet, Inc.
Eastman Kodak Co.
Ebasco International Corp.
Elizabeth Arden Corp.
First National City Bank
General Electric Co.
General Motors Corp.
General Telephone & Electronics
   Corp.
Gillette Co.
B. F. Goodrich Co.
International Business Machines
   Corp.
International Petroleum Co.,
   Ltd.
Liquid Carbonic Division
Manpower Inc.
McCann–Erickson, Inc.
McKesson & Robbins, Inc.
Mead Johnson & Co.
Merck & Co., Inc.
Minneapolis-Moline Corp.
National Cash Register Co.
National Cylinder Gas Division
Otis Elevator Co.
Phelps Dodge Corp.
Price, Waterhouse & Co.
Quaker Oats International Co.
Seiberling Rubber Co.
Singer Co., Inc.
Sperry Rand Corp.
E. R. Squibb & Sons Division
Standard Brands, Inc.
Texaco, Inc.
Todd Shipyards Corp.
Union Carbide Corp.
United States Rubber Co.
Warner Bros. Pictures Inter-
   national Corp.
Warner-Lambert Pharmaceutical
   Co.
Westinghouse Electric Corp.

DENMARK
Airtool Manufacturing Co.
American Express Co.
Bendix Aviation Corp.
Burroughs Corp.
Chesebrough-Ponds, Inc.
Colgate-Palmolive International,
   Inc.
Corn Products Refining Co.
Eastman Kodak Co.
Ford Motor Co.
General Motors Corp.
Gillette Co.
Goodyear Tire & Rubber Co.
Gulf Oil Corp.
International Business Machines
   Corp.
International Harvester Co.
International Telephone & Tele-
   graph Corp.
International Tobacco Co.
Manpower Inc.
Metro-Goldwyn-Mayer, Inc.
National Cash Register Co.
Quaker Oats International Co.
Singer Co., Inc.
Socony Mobil Oil Co., Inc.
Standard Oil Co.
Western Electric Co., Inc.

FRANCE
Abbott Laboratories Inter-
   national
Addressograph-Multigraph Corp.
Airtool Manufacturing Co.
American Brake Shoe Co.
American Standard Corp.
Blaw-Knox Co.
Burroughs Corp.
Chicago Pneumatic Tool Co.
Cities Service Oil Co.
Coca-Cola Co.

Colgate-Palmolive International, Inc.
Combustion Engineering, Inc.
Coty International Corp.
Crown Cork and Seal Corp.
Dana Corp.
Eastman Kodak Co.
Eimco Corp.
Ford Motor Co.
Gillette Co.
B. F. Goodrich Co.
International Business Machines Corp.
International Harvester Co.
International Paper Co.
Manpower Inc.
National Lead Co.
Pepsi-Cola Co.
Richardson-Merrell, Inc.
Socony Mobil Oil Co., Inc.
Sperry Rand Corp.
E. R. Squibb & Sons Division
Standard Oil Co. of California
Standard Oil Co. of New Jersey
Worthington Corp.

GERMANY

Airtool Manufacturing Co.
American Foreign Insurance Association
American Independence Life Insurance Co.
American International Underwriters Corp.
American Standard Corp.
Amperex, Inc.
Armco Steel Corp.
Bank of America
Budd Co.
Burroughs Corp.
Canada Dry International, Inc.
Carborundum Co.
Cargill, Inc.

Celanese Corp. of America
Chase Manhattan Bank
Chicago Pneumatic Tool Co.
Clevite Corp.
Coca-Cola Co.
Colgate-Palmolive International, Inc.
Container Corp. of America
Corn Products Refining Co.
Walt Disney Productions, Inc.
Dun and Bradstreet, Inc.
E. I. du Pont de Nemours & Co.
Eastman Kodak Co.
Firestone Tire & Rubber Co.
First National City Bank
Ford Motor Co.
General Foods Corp.
General Motors Corp.
Gillette Co.
Goodyear Tire & Rubber Co.
Gulf Oil Corp.
Hoffman Machinery Distributors, Inc.
Home Insurance Co.
Honeywell International Division
Hudson Hosiery Co.
International Business Machines Corp.
International Finance Corp.
International Harvester Co.
International Telephone & Telegraph Corp.
Intertype Corp.
Walter Kidde & Co., Inc.
Koppers Co., Inc.
Lederle Laboratories
Lehn & Fink Products Corp.
Libby, McNeill & Libby
Manpower Inc.
Marchant Calculator Division
McCann-Erickson, Inc.
McGraw-Hill, Inc.
Mergenthaler Linotype Co.

Minnesota Mining & Manufacturing Co.
National Cash Register Co.
National Lead Co.
North European Oil Corp.
Olivetti Underwood Corp.
Otis Elevator Co.
Pepsi-Cola Co.
Perkin-Elmer Corp.
Pfaudler Permutit, Inc.
Pioneer American Insurance
Price, Waterhouse & Co.
Quaker Oats International Co.
School Manufacturing Co., Inc.
Singer Co., Inc.
Standard Oil Co. of New Jersey
Stanley Works
Swift & Co.
J. Walter Thompson Co.
Transatlantic Pigment Corp.
Underwood Corp.
United States Rubber Co.
Warner-Lambert Pharmaceutical Co.
Wilson & Co., Inc.
F. W. Woolworth Co.
Wm. Wrigley, Jr. Co.
Young & Rubicam, Inc.

GREAT BRITAIN

Abbott Laboratories International
Addressograph-Multigraph Corp.
American Home Products Corp.
American Laundry Machinery Industries
American Standard Corp.
Armour & Co.
Armstrong Cork Co., Inc.
ASR Products Co.
Bankers Trust Co.
Blaw-Knox Co.

Borg-Warner International Corp.
Bristol-Myers Co.
Bucyrus-Erie Co.
Burroughs Corp.
Champion Spark Plug Co.
Chesebrough-Ponds, Inc.
Chrysler Corp.
Colgate-Palmolive International, Inc.
Coty International Corp.
Crane Co.
Crown Cork & Seal Corp.
Cutler-Hammer, Inc.
Dana Corp.
Daystrom, Inc.
Eastman Kodak Co.
Thomas A. Edison Industries
Eimco Corp.
First National City Bank
Firestone Tire & Rubber Co.
Ford Motor Co.
General Electric Co.
General Motors Corp.
General Time Corp.
Gillette Co.
B. F. Goodrich Co.
Goodyear Tire & Rubber Co.
Gulf Oil Corp.
H. J. Heinz Co.
Honeywell International Division
International Business Machines Corp.
International Harvester Co.
International Packers, Ltd.
International Paper Co.
Johns-Manville Corp.
Johnson & Johnson
Joy Manufacturing Co.
Libby, McNeill & Libby
Lincoln Electric Co.
Liquid Carbonic Corp.
Manpower Inc.
Mergenthaler Linotype Co.

Monsanto Chemical Co.
National Biscuit Co.
National Dairy Products Corp.
National Lead Co.
Parke, Davis & Co.
Pepsi-Cola Co.
Philco Corp.
Quaker Oats International Co.
Richardson-Merrell, Inc.
Ruberoid Co.
St. Regis Paper Co.
Scovill Manufacturing Co.
Simmons Co.
Sperry Rand Corp.
E. R. Squibb & Sons Division
Standard Brands, Inc.
Standard Oil Co. of California
Standard Oil Co. of New Jersey
Sterling Drug Co.
Sylvania Electric Products, Inc.
Texaco, Inc.
United Engineering & Foundry
   Co.
Wm. Wrigley, Jr., Co.
York Corp.

GREECE

Abbott Laboratories Inter-
   national
American Tobacco Co.
California Texas Oil Corp.
Ebasco International Corp.
R. J. Reynolds Tobacco Co.
Singer Co., Inc.
Thompson & Merritt

ISRAEL

Abbott Laboratories Interna-
   tional
Admiral Corp.
Bendix Corp.
Caterpillar Tractors Co., Inc.
Coca-Cola Co.

Cott Industries, Inc.
Dun and Bradstreet, Inc.
Eastman Kodak Co.
Firestone Tire & Rubber Co.
Ford Motor Co.
General Motors Corp.
General Shoe Corp.
General Tire & Rubber Co.
National Cash Register Co.
Pepsi-Cola Co.
Singer Co., Inc.
Standard Brands, Inc.
Standard Oil Co. of New Jersey
Texaco, Inc.
Westinghouse Electric Corp.

ITALY

Abbott Laboratories Interna-
   tional
Admiral Corp.
American Foreign Insurance
   Association
American Home Products Corp.
American International Under-
   writers Corp.
American Standard Corp.
Armco Steel Corp.
Associated Merchandising Corp.
Associated Metals & Minerals
   Corp.
Automatic Electric Sales Co.
Chase Manhattan Bank
Coca-Cola Co.
Colgate-Palmolive International,
   Inc.
Continental Grain Co.
Corn Products Refining Co.
Coty International Corp.
Eastman Kodak Co.
Elizabeth Arden Corp.
Ford Motor Co.
General Analine & Film Corp.
General Electric Co.

Gulf Oil Corp.
International Business Machines
    Corp.
International Standard Electric
    Corp.
Lehman Brothers
Marshall Field & Co.
Max Factor & Co.
Mergenthaler Linotype Co.
Morrison-Knudsen Co., Inc.
National Cash Register Co.
Norton International, Inc.
Otis Elevator Co.
Parke, Davis & Co.
Philco International Corp.
Procter & Gamble Distributing
    Co.
Reichhold Chemicals, Inc.
Republic Pictures International
    Co.
Rexall Drug Co.
Shell Oil Co.
Singer Co., Inc.
Sperry Rand Corp.
Standard Oil Co. of New Jersey
Syracuse Smelting Works
J. Walter Thompson Co.
Trans World Airlines, Inc.
Union Carbide Corp.
Van Raalte Co., Inc.
Warner-Lambert Pharmaceutical
    Co.
Westinghouse Air Brake Co.

JAPAN

Bank of America
First National City Bank
International Business Machines
    Corp.
Johns-Manville Corp.
Manpower Inc.

Max Factor & Co.
Pepsi-Cola Co.

MEXICO

American Metals Co.
American Smelting & Refining
    Co.
American Standard Corp.
Anderson, Clayton & Co.
Armco Steel Corp.
Brunswick Corp.
Burroughs Corp.
Celanese Corp. of America
Chase Manhattan Bank
Chrysler Corp.
Coca-Cola Co.
Colgate-Palmolive International,
    Inc.
Corn Products Refining Co.
E. I. du Pont de Nemours & Co.
Eagle-Picher Co.
Eastman Kodak Co.
First National City Bank
General Motors Corp.
General Tire & Rubber Co.
B. F. Goodrich Co.
Goodyear Tire & Rubber Co.
Intercontinental Rubber Co.
International Business Machines
    Corp.
International Harvester Co.
Manpower Inc.
National Cash Register Co.
National Lead Co.
Nestle Co., Inc.
Pepsi-Cola Co.
Phelps Dodge Corp.
Reynolds Metals Co.
Sherwin-Williams Co.
Standard Gas & Electric Co.,
    Inc.

Union Carbide Corp.
Westinghouse Electric Corp.

NETHERLANDS
American Chicle Corp.
American Standard Corp.
Anderson, Clayton & Co.
Arabian American Oil Co.
Borden Co.
Burroughs Corp.
Coca-Cola Co.
Chicago Pneumatic Tool Co.
Colgate-Palmolive International, Inc.
Combustion Engineering, Inc.
Continental Can Co.
Controls Co. of America
Corn Products Refining Co.
Crane Co.
Curtiss-Wright Corp.
Dow Chemical Co.
Dun and Bradstreet, Inc.
Eastman Kodak Co.
Fairchild Camera & Instrument Corp.
Fairchild Engine & Airplane Corp.
Felt & Tarrant Manufacturing Co.
Ferro Corp.
Fischer & Porter Co.
Ford Motor Co.
Friden, Inc.
General Motors Corp.
General Tire & Rubber Co.
B. F. Goodrich Co.
Gulf Oil Corp.
Hewitt-Robins, Inc.
Hobart Manufacturing Co.
Honeywell International Division
International Business Machines Co.

International Standard Electric Corp.
Kraft Foods Division
Manpower Inc.
Monroe Calculating Machine Co., Inc.
National Cash Register Co.
Olivetti Underwood Corp.
Otis Elevator Co.
Pepsi-Cola Co.
Price, Waterhouse & Co.
Quaker Oats International Co.
Quaker State Oil Refining Corp.
Royal McBee Corp.
Signode Corp.
Sperry Rand Corp.
Standard Oil Co. of New Jersey
Standard Vacuum Oil Co.
Sun Oil Co.
Swift & Co.
Texas Instruments Inc.
Textile Machinery Works
United Fruit Co.

NEW ZEALAND
Abbott Laboratories International
American Home Products Corp.
Bristol-Myers Co.
Colgate-Palmolive International, Inc.
Firestone Tire & Rubber Co.
Ford Motor Co.
B. F. Goodrich Co.
International Packers, Ltd.
Johnson & Johnson
Liquid Carbonic Corp.
Richardson-Merrell, Inc.
Standard Oil Co. of California
Standard Oil Co. of New Jersey
Sterling Drug Co.

Texaco, Inc.
Wm. Wrigley, Jr., Co.

PANAMA

American & Foreign Power Co.,
Inc.
Chase Manhattan Bank
Colgate-Palmolive International,
Inc.
Container Corp. of America
Coty International Corp.
First National City Bank
Manpower Inc.
Parke, Davis & Co.
Pepsi-Cola Co.
Standard Oil Co. of New Jersey
Texaco, Inc.
Union Oil Co. of California
United States Gypsum Co.
United States Plywood Corp.

PORTUGAL

Abbott Laboratories Inter-
national
Armstrong Cork Co., Inc.
Colgate-Palmolive International,
Inc.
Crown Cork and Seal Corp.
Dun and Bradstreet, Inc.
Eastman Kodak Co.
Ford Motor Co.
General Electric Co.
General Motors Corp.
General Tire & Rubber Co.
Ingersoll-Rand Co.
International Business Machines
Corp.
Manpower Inc.
National Cash Register Co.
Price, Waterhouse & Co.

Singer Co., Inc.
Socony Mobil Oil Co., Inc.
Standard Oil Co. of New Jersey
United States Steel Corp.

SPAIN

Abbott Laboratories Interna-
tional
American Cyanamid Co.
Armour & Co.
Armstrong Cork Co., Inc.
Atlantic Refining Co.
Babcock & Wilcox Co.
California Texas Oil Corp.
Coca-Cola Co.
Colgate-Palmolive International,
Inc.
Dun and Bradstreet, Inc.
Eastman Kodak Co.
Elizabeth Arden Co.
Firestone Tire & Rubber Co.
Fruehauf Trailer Division
General Motors Corp.
General Tire & Rubber Co.
H. J. Heinz Co.
International Business Machines
Corp.
International General Electric
Co.
International Harvester Co.
International Telephone & Tele-
graph Corp.
National Cash Register Co.
New Hampshire Insurance Co.
Orange Crush Co.
Singer Co., Inc.
Sperry Rand Corp.
Standard Oil Co. of New Jersey
Texaco, Inc.
Union Oil & Gas Corp. of
Louisiana

Warner-Lambert Pharmaceutical
Co.
Westinghouse Air Brake Co.
Westinghouse International Co.

SWEDEN

Abbott Laboratories International
American Standard Corp.
Bausch & Lomb, Inc.
California Texas Oil Corp.
Coca-Cola Co.
Colgate-Palmolive International, Inc.
Ford Motor Co.
General Motors Corp.
Gillette Co.
B. F. Goodrich Co.
Goodyear Tire & Rubber Co.
Gulf Oil Corp.
Honeywell International Division
International Business Machines Corp.
International Harvester Co.
Metro-Goldwyn-Mayer, Inc.
National Cash Register Co.
Pfizer International, Inc.
Quaker Oats International Co.
Singer Co., Inc.
Sperry Rand Corp.
Standard Electric Corp.
Standard Oil Co. of New Jersey
Union Carbide Corp.

SWITZERLAND

Abbott Laboratories International
Allis-Chalmers Manufacturing Co.

American Standard Corp.
Colgate-Palmolive International, Inc.
Firestone Tire & Rubber Co.
General Motors Corp.
Gillette Co.
Honeywell International Division
Manpower Inc.
Standard Oil Co. of New Jersey

TURKEY

Abbott Laboratories International
American Tobacco Co.
California Texas Oil Corp.
Eastman Kodak Co.
Foster Wheeler Corp.
General Electric Co.
International Business Machines Corp.
Liggett & Myers Tobacco Co.
R. H. Macy & Co.
Manpower Inc.
Minneapolis-Moline Co.
Morrison-Knudsen Co., Inc.
National Cash Register Co.
Singer Co., Inc.
E. R. Squibb & Sons Division
Standard Oil Co. of New Jersey

SOUTH AFRICA

Abbott Laboratories International
American Cyanamid Co.
American Home Products Corp.
American Metals Co.
Armstrong Cork Co., Inc.
Borden Co.
Bristol-Myers Co.
Chesebrough-Ponds, Inc.

Chicago Pneumatic Tool Co.
Coca-Cola Co.
Colgate-Palmolive International,
    Inc.
Crown Cork and Seal Corp.
Firestone Tire & Rubber Co.
Ford Motor Co.
General Electric Co.
General Tire & Rubber Co.
Goodyear Tire & Rubber Co.
International Packers, Ltd.
Johnson & Johnson
Joy Manufacturing Co.
Kellogg Co.
Link-Belt Co.
Liquid Carbonic Division
Manpower Inc.
Procter & Gamble Distributing
    Co.
Richardson-Merrell, Inc.
Sperry Rand Corp.
Standard Brands International
    Corp.
Standard Oil Co. of California
Standard Oil Co. of New Jersey
Standard Vacuum Oil Co.
Sterling Drug Co.
Texaco, Inc.

VENEZUELA
Abbott Laboratories Inter-
    national
American Chicle Co.
American Foreign Insurance
    Association
American & Foreign Power Co.,
    Inc.
American International Under-
    writers Corp.
Atlantic Refining Co.
Bethlehem Steel Corp.

Burroughs Corp.
Celanese Corp. of America
Colgate-Palmolive International,
    Inc.
Cooper-Bessemer Corp.
Firestone Tire & Rubber Co.
First National City Bank
General Motors Corp.
General Tire & Rubber Co.
Goodyear Rubber & Tire Co.
Grant Advertising, Inc.
Gulf Oil Corp.
Insurance Co. of North America
International General Electric
    Co.
Lane-Wells Co.
Liquid Carbonic Division
Manpower Inc.
McCann-Erickson, Inc.
McWilliams Dredging Co.
Merritt-Chapman & Scott Corp.
Morrison-Knudsen Co., Inc.
National Biscuit Co.
National Cash Register Co.
National Cylinder Gas Division
National Paper & Type Co.
National Union Fire Insurance
    Co.
Otis Elevator Co.
Pan American Life Insurance
    Co.
Parke, Davis & Co.
Pfizer International, Inc.
Phillips Petroleum Co.
Price, Waterhouse & Co.
Procter & Gamble Distributing
    Co.
Raymond Concrete Pile Division
Sinclair Refining Co.
Singer Co., Inc.
Sperry Rand Corp.
E. R. Squibb & Sons Division

Standard Brands International Corp.

Standard Oil Co. of California

Standard Oil Co. of New Jersey

Texaco, Inc.

Union Bag-Camp Paper Corp.

United Merchants & Manufacturers, Inc.

United States Life Insurance Co.

United States Rubber Co.

Westinghouse Electric Co.

CHAPTER XI

Government Jobs

"You've dreamed of faraway places—Bangkok, New Delhi, Ankara. Or perhaps your dreams have gone further—away from the beaten track—Katmandu—Djakarta—Addis Ababa—Lagos."

Sound like a travel brochure? It isn't. It is a quotation from a pamphlet published by the Agency for International Development of the U.S. State Department.

The pamphlet, designed to recruit secretaries for the agency, begins: "You are a secretary—or a stenographer. You're a bit tired of the dull routine—you want a more challenging outlook—a chance to take part in the history-making programs under way to improve world conditions."

It sounds irresistible for anyone with secretarial skills, and it could be your ticket to travel with pay for the United States government.

The variety of skills needed in overseas positions with the government is almost unlimited. The list includes maintenance and construction workers, doctors, nurses, teachers, technical experts, mining engineers, social workers, typists, geologists—all working for Uncle Sam.

You could work as a civilian employee of one of the military services, of the Departments of State, Commerce, or Agriculture, or of the United States Information Agency. And then, of course, there is the new and exciting work being done by the Peace Corps volunteers.

Let us talk briefly about some of the general conditions of government employment before going into specific information regarding each field.

You must be at least twenty-one years old and in excellent health to be considered for overseas appointments. Because you might serve under extremely difficult living conditions, and because some areas do not have complete medical facilities, you and all dependents accompanying you will be required to pass rigid physical examinations. You must also meet standards of mental and emotional stability and maturity.

Employment with the government makes you subject to security, character, and suitability investigations. If you are eligible for the draft, you must have written permission from your draft board to leave the country. However, if you have already had military service, you would be given extra consideration for an overseas position under the provisions of the Veterans' Preference Act.

Because the shortage of housing for government employees abroad is often acute, there are usually waiting lists for dependent housing. If you intend to have dependents accompany you, therefore, you should be prepared for a separation of about a year. Appointments of husband and wife at the same post are rare, because there are seldom simultaneous openings in which the qualifications of both can be used.

You would be expected to stay abroad for a minimum of two years, although in some posts of difficult or hazardous living conditions the minimum period is 12 or 18 months.

The general qualifications for overseas jobs are roughly the same as for similar jobs in this country except that the standards might be higher.

Your salary as a white-collar worker would have the same base as the salaries paid to Federal employees in the United States. In addition, you would receive a post differential, a cost-of-living allowance, or both, depending on the conditions at the post to which you were assigned. These allowances are designed to equalize the purchasing power of your salary. Blue-collar workers' wages are based upon rates paid in the United States plus, in some cases, the post differential and cost-of-living allowance.

Government employees are often housed in government-owned or -rented quarters. If such housing is not available, a housing allowance is paid to white-collar workers to cover rent and utilities.

Government overseas employees are eligible for Federal employee benefits, which include paid vacations, sick leave with pay, and retirement coverage. They are also eligible for life insurance and health benefits, partially paid for by the government.

Overseas employees are provided free transportation for themselves and their dependents, transportation or storage for their household goods, and additional paid vacations with free travel home between tours of duty. In many areas the government operates schools for dependents, which are often comparable to the better schools in the United States.

What kind of job might you hold as a civilian employee of the government? This varies with the department or agency for which you work. Let us examine them one at a time.

Civilian Jobs with the Military Services

Many overseas jobs with the Department of the Army are filled through reassignment of Army career employees. However, openings exist for persons with specialized skills. Civilian employees include librarians, cartographers, recreation specialists, teachers, and engineers. Teaching vacancies often occur in elementary and secondary schools for Army dependents.

Since civilian jobs with the Army, except for school staff jobs, require Civil Service status, your first step would be to take a competitive examination. Your local Post Office can tell you when and where these examinations are given.

Overseas commands are authorized to hire persons already overseas who are not within reach of Civil Service examining boards and thus do not have Civil Service status, but these openings are rare. Don't go overseas expecting to find a job with the Army just by presenting yourself, but if you are already abroad and looking for a job, you might happen to be on hand when a vacancy in your field of work occurs.

Inquiries about jobs with the Army should be addressed to:

Interchange and Recruitment Coordination Branch
Employee Management Division
OCP, DCSPER
Department of the Army
Washington, D.C. 20310

Employment with the Department of the Navy falls in the same general fields as with the Army. To teach in a Navy dependents' school, you must be twenty-three years old and must apply before March 1 for the following school year.

College graduates with a background of study in international relations, political science, history, and geography are sometimes hired for work in Navy intelligence, if there are not enough regular Navy personnel to fill the positions.

Most civilian jobs with the Navy are in the Pacific area. If you would like to work for the Navy in the Pacific, write:

> Navy Overseas Employment Office (Pacific)
> Federal Office Building
> San Francisco, California

For other overseas jobs with the Navy, write:

> Navy Overseas Employment Office (Atlantic) Headquarters
> Potomac River Naval Command
> Washington, D.C. 20390

Employment opportunities with the Air Force are largely in engineering, teaching, accounting, recreation, and library work. Employees from Air Force installations in the United States are given primary consideration for overseas work.

The minimum tour of duty with the Air Force is two years, except in the Azores, Aleutians, Guam, Arabia, and Okinawa, where the tour is 12 to 18 months.

Inquiries should be addressed to:

> Air Force Overseas Employment Office
> Building 410, Room 2007
> Bolling Air Force Base
> Washington, D.C.

Department of Agriculture

Specialists in agricultural marketing and agricultural economics can often qualify for well-paying jobs with the U.S. Department of Agriculture Foreign Agricultural Service (FAS). Generally appointments are made from the Federal service entrance examination and Civil Service examinations for agricultural economist and agricultural marketing specialist.

Some secretarial positions are filled from the list of eligibles in the clerk-stenographic examination of the Civil Service Commission, but usually these positions are filled by persons already employed by the department.

You can get additional information by writing:

Personnel Division
Foreign Agricultural Service
Department of Agriculture
Washington, D.C. 20250

Department of Commerce

Four bureaus within the Commerce Department employ overseas personnel in highly specialized fields.

The Bureau of Public Roads employs highway and bridge engineers, specialists in administration and supervision of road-construction equipment, and people with experience in planning construction and maintenance of roads. If you have experience in one of these fields and are interested in possible work overseas with the Department of Commerce, write to:

Bureau of Public Roads
Washington, D.C. 20235

Engineers and physicists with experience in operation and maintenance of radar, guided missiles, and other electronic systems can work for the National Bureau of Standards.

If you have always wanted to see the frozen wonders of the Antarctic, you can spend 12 to 18 months there as an employee of the bureau.

Inquiries should be addressed to:

Personnel Officer
National Bureau of Standards
Boulder Laboratories
Boulder, Colorado

Weather stations in such varied locations as Hawaii and the Antarctic are maintained by the Weather Bureau. You should have experience in meteorology or electronics to apply. Information can be obtained from:

U.S. Weather Bureau
Washington, D.C. 20235

If you have experience in the highly technical field of geophysics, you might find an overseas job with the Coast and Geodetic Survey. Write for information to:

Director
Coast and Geodetic Survey
Washington, D.C. 20230

Department of the Interior
Strange as it may seem, this branch of government is also a source of overseas jobs. The Department of the Interior is the principal natural resources agency for the continental United States, but it also is responsible for the administration and public welfare of island possessions in the Caribbean and the South Pacific. The department also has guardianship over 400,000 Indians, including 34,000 Indians, Eskimos, and Aleuts in Alaska.

Following are some of the job opportunities with the Department of the Interior outside the continental United States.

The Bureau of Reclamation employs engineers, power plant operators, linemen, laborers, and administrative and clerical personnel in its offices in Juneau and Anchorage, Alaska. For information write to:

Director
Bureau of Reclamation
Juneau, Alaska

Specialists in the technical aspects of mining might find work with the Bureau of Mines, which operates in Alaska and in cooperation with foreign projects assigned by other government agencies. For information on foreign mining assignments with the bureau, write to:

Chief, Division of International Activities
Bureau of Mines
Department of the Interior
Washington, D.C. 20240

If you are interested in working for the Bureau of Mines in Alaska, address your inquiries to:

Area Director, Area 8
Mineral Resource Office
Juneau, Alaska

The Bureau of Land Management directs the survey, management, and disposition of public lands in Alaska. Occasionally it has openings for foresters, agricultural economists, conservation specialists, realty officers, draftsmen, and administrative personnel. Inquiries should be directed to:

Field Administrative Officer
Bureau of Land Management
Box 3861
Portland, Oregon 97208

The Bureau of Indian Affairs employs teachers, social workers, general clerical and administrative personnel, mechanics, and cooks. Write for information to:

Area Director
Bureau of Indian Affairs
Juneau, Alaska

The Office of the Territories administers American Samoa, Guam, the Virgin Islands, and the Trust Territory of the Pacific Islands, but only in the last named area is there much opportunity for government employment. The Trust Territory encompasses an area about the size of the United States, made up of the Mariana, Caroline, and Marshall islands. The islands have a population of nearly 85,000, most of whom are Micronesians.

The Department of the Interior administers the islands under a trusteeship agreement between the United States and the United Nations. The stated aims are to develop the people of the Trust Territory so that they can assume the responsibilities of self-government, to make them economically self-sufficient, and to foster respect for their cultures while affording them an opportunity to adopt those aspects of Western life which will enable them to live richer lives.

Judging from the number of brochures and pamphlets printed for prospective government employees of the Trust Territory, the department is engaged in active recruiting. The work force of Americans consists primarily of specialists in agriculture, education, medicine, and general administration and is appointed under Civil Service procedures.

The tour of duty in the Trust Territory is two years, and salaries are subject to a post differential (currently 20 per cent). One reason for the differential may be the climate, which is warm (average daily temperature about 80 degrees) and humid. The Marshall Islands have an annual rainfall of about 120 inches. Another reason is a "certain deprivation of 20th-century amenities: Selection on trading company shelves is often spotty, general stores are considered good if they do not run out of staple items too often, there is only one movie or one or two clubs to go to in an evening, air mail arrives weekly and surface mail approximately once a month, you cannot jump into your car and drive more than a few miles to get a change of scene, etc."

But there is challenge and potential in the Trust Territory of which many Americans looking for jobs abroad are unaware. If you are tired of the bustle of American life and of long, cold winters, perhaps you would like to escape to the South Pacific, where your work could be exciting as well as meaningful. For more information write to:

Personnel Officer
Government of the Trust Territory of the Pacific Islands
Saipan, Mariana Islands.

Department of State

It is to the giant U.S. Department of State that most civilian employees look for government jobs abroad. The government is the largest single employer of Americans overseas, and most of its jobs are with the State Department.

The department maintains three hundred posts in more than one hundred countries and has a continuing need for secretaries, stenographers, and communications and record clerks to staff its embassies, legations, and consulates.

The Foreign Service Staff Corps is one of three branches of the foreign service. Well over half of its members are women, who serve as clerks, typists, code clerks, stenographers, and in special administrative jobs.

The second and best-known group of posts in the State Department are those of the Foreign Service officers. This professional career corps has about 3,400 members, of whom some 300 are women, and with these people rests the main work of the service. They conduct the diplomatic and consular affairs of the United States and represent its government to the governments of other countries. They negotiate treaties and other agreements and protect the interests and welfare of American citizens on foreign soil. They issue passports, participate in cultural and educational exchange activities, and protect and promote American commercial interests abroad.

There are four stages in the selection of Foreign Service officers and reserve officers, a competitive written examination, an oral examination, a medical examination, and a background investigation.

The written examination, which is given twice a year in most large cities, consists of five tests, which take a total of six hours and fifteen minutes to complete.

The first test is one of general ability to read, analyze, and interpret tabular and quantitative data. In addition to questions relating to text, maps, tables, and graphs, it poses such questions as these:[1]

1. The epigrammatic style of the book gives it an appearance of _____ which is somewhat deceptive, for the argument is developed so tersely that it is not always easy to follow.
   a. Lucidity
   b. Erudition
   c. Complexity
   d. Accuracy
   e. Mysticism
2. On the one hand scientific research introduces new methods of _____; on the other it invents new devices to _____ their effects.
   a. Production . . . implement
   b. Observation . . . reduce
   c. Destruction . . . counteract
   d. Warfare . . . increase
   e. Experimentation . . . enhance

[1] Answers: 1. A; 2. C; 3. D; 4. D; 5. D; 6. B.

3. If 30 new Pullman cars seat as many people as 39 old Pullman cars, by what per cent has the seating capacity of each Pullman car been increased?
   a. 3 b. 9 c. 25 d. 30 e. 33⅓

The first part of the test of English expression involves revising a poorly written passage. Another part asks you to divide a passage into the central idea, main supporting ideas, illustrative facts, and irrelevant statements. The last part asks you to choose the most appropriate answer for a given situation or incident.

4. Which one of the following sentences is most appropriately worded for inclusion in an impartial report resulting from an investigation of a wage policy in a certain locality?
   a. The wages of the working people are fixed by the one businessman who is the only large employer in the locality.
   b. Since one employer provides a livelihood for the entire population in the locality, he properly determines the wage policy for the locality.
   c. Since one employer controls the labor market in a locality, his policy may not be challenged.
   d. In this locality, where there is only one large employer of labor, the wage policy of this employer is really the wage policy of the locality.

In the third test of the written examination, you are required to spend one hour writing an essay on a subject from a list of ten or twelve. Logic, grammatical structure, clarity, and readability are major factors in grading the essay. Two sample topics are:

Why is the United States economic aid to underdeveloped areas important in relation to its political objectives? Discuss.
What characteristics or qualities of your country would you be most proud of in representing it abroad?

The fourth test is one of general background. It includes such questions as the following:

5. In the middle of the twentieth century, political boundaries of Africa were determined by:
   a. geographic realities

  b. economic factors
  c. tribal organization
  d. 19th-century European power politics
  e. nationalist sentiments
 6. What would be the probable type of musical program devoted solely to the compositions of Mahler, Beethoven, Shostakovitch, and Hindemith?
  a. Piano recital
  b. Symphony orchestra concert
  c. String quartet recital
  d. Organ concert
  e. Song recital

In the fifth and last test of the written examination, you may choose one of four options on which to be tested.

Option A: History, social sciences, government and public affairs. (All candidates for positions as foreign service officers with the United States Information Agency must choose Option A.)
Option B: Administration
Option C: Economics
Option D: Commerce

The examinations are graded "on the curve," a system familiar to most students. If you answered 50 per cent of the questions correctly and no one else scored higher, you would receive top score for that examination.

It might be noted that there is no test for language skills. After you enter the foreign service, however, a language test is required following your in-service training program. More than 30 languages are useful to the department, and it has a program for positive recognition —presumably higher pay—for persons possessing language skills.

The oral examination, which lasts about an hour and a half, is conducted by a panel of experienced officers. The purpose of the test is to measure the candidate's personal qualities, resourcefulness, and versatility, the breadth and depth of his interests, his ability to work with people and to express and defend his views in the presence of a well-informed group, and his general suitability to be a representative of the United States abroad.

When a candidate has progressed this far, he is given a thorough medical examination, since many Foreign Service posts require more than average endurance and vitality.

During this time a background investigation is made to ensure the government that the candidate can be trusted with the responsibilities that will be imposed upon him.

The candidate who successfully passes all of these tests will be offered employment and will be assigned to the junior officer program for on-the-job training at the Foreign Service Institute in Washington, D.C. Thereafter he will receive his first overseas assignment as a secretary in the diplomatic service or as a vice-consul.

As we have seen in Chapter VI, a beginning officer earns from $5,540 to $6,650 annually in Class 8 and can work up to Class 1 as a career ambassador at a salary of $20,000.

The third branch of the Foreign Service comprises the reserve officers, persons with highly specialized skills such as Soviet agriculture, Arabic culture, or the petroleum industry. Reserve officers work under much the same conditions as do the career officers, except that they serve for five-year periods.

Inquiries about working in the Foreign Service Staff Corps should be addressed to:

Employment Division
Department of State
Washington, D.C. 20520

If you are between twenty-one and thirty-one years of age and would like to consider a career as a Foreign Service officer, write to:

Board of Examiners for the Foreign Service
Department of State
Washington, D.C. 20520

One of the lesser known jobs with the State Department is that of diplomatic courier. These are the men—sorry, no women allowed—who carry confidential correspondence in sealed pouches from one diplomatic post to another.

This is an ideal opportunity for an unmarried college graduate who is fluent in a language other than English and would like to spend two years traveling abroad.

One young applicant, tired of his desk job in a major American city, filled out Standard Form 57, available at the local Post Office, and sent it to the State Department. For three months he heard nothing, but one day he answered the telephone and found a State Department official on the line. He had received an appointment and was wanted in Washington by the end of the week! He told the official that he had to give two weeks' notice at his present job and that he would report in a month. Finally, after bargaining reminiscent of an Oriental market, he agreed to be there in three weeks.

He reported in due course and underwent ten days of training, then spent a weekend at home saying goodbye to his family and friends. "And then," he said, "there I was, carrying mail for Uncle Sam."

Agency for International Development (A.I.D.)

This agency is the principal administrator of America's economic and technical aid to the underdeveloped countries of the world. Highly specialized skills are needed in agriculture, engineering, public health, education and public administration, economics, housing, and other fields.

In addition to technical skills, A.I.D. people must have patience to carry them through frustrating times, a belief in the program and its ultimate goals, and a sensitivity to other people and their problems.

In addition to persons with technical skills, the agency also employs secretaries. It was from the brochure to recruit secretaries for the A.I.D. that we quoted at the beginning of this chapter. This intriguing pamphlet goes on: "You will work for a prestige organization and share in the biggest job being attempted today, that of building world peace. As a member of such a team you will find yourself a real participant in a great world effort."

To qualify you must be over twenty-one years of age, a high-school graduate, an American citizen, unmarried, and in good health. For Grade 10 (the minimum requirement), you must be able to type 50 words a minute, take shorthand at 80 words a minute, and have three years of office experience (or equivalent combination-education beyond high school).

On the job you must show no racial, religious, or national prejudices nor be critical of the host country, its government, or its living conditions.

A secretary from Chicago, who had spent two years working in the

American Embassy in Berne, Switzerland, became intrigued with Nepal and was delighted when her application for transfer was accepted. Because Nepal is a small country, it was easy to get acquainted. In fact, she counted some of the royal family among her friends and occasionally used the royal plane for trips to Calcutta. She learned to shoot and has a tiger-skin rug to prove it. She was included in Nepalese parties and entertainment and played baseball with the natives when they were guests at American picnics. After Nepal, she worked in Rio de Janeiro, Brazil, and Ankara, Turkey, and admits that she now understands foreign attitudes better than American ones.

Although she is currently based in Washington, she will probably go abroad again. She says, "There is too much to see, too many people to meet, for me to settle down now."

Your job with the A.I.D. overseas will not be a vacation at government expense, however. It will be hard work, probably harder than anything you are doing at home. You may have to live in primitive conditions and endure high temperatures, humidity, dust, and insects. But if you have stamina, patience, responsibility, and a strong sense of humor, this may be the job for you.

Further information on jobs with the Agency for International Development may be obtained from:

> Director, Office of Personnel Administration
> Box CS-1
> Agency for International Development
> Department of State
> Washington, D.C. 20523

Central Intelligence Agency (C.I.A.)

Within the covers of the latest spy story looms the large but cloudy outline of the supersecret Central Intelligence Agency. Even the President is unaware of exactly how many people are employed by the C.I.A. and of its total operating budget, which is buried in the miscellaneous funds of hundreds of other government organizations.

The fact that it is large can be seen by looking at the building in Washington, D.C., marked, however discreetly, with the agency's name. But daily hundreds of people pass the security guards and spend their days working for the Central Intelligence Agency.

At what? Well, secretaries and file clerks process reports from all over the world. Then there are specialists in explosives, mapmaking, parachuting, and other fields not only too numerous but also too secret to mention.

Take, for example, the university professor who preferred recreation to research and was denied tenure under the current "publish or perish" policy. Where is he now? In Washington working for the C.I.A. His colleagues at the university admit that they don't know just what he is doing. But this university professor was born in China, the son of missionary parents, and his major field of study was Far Eastern affairs.

How about you? Would it be necessary for you to be a specialist in a particular part of the world to be employed by the C.I.A.? No, but you would have to be a specialist in something. For an overseas job with the C.I.A. you would certainly have to be at least bilingual.

You must be the epitome of the Boy Scout—and also be a good liar. You must be able to go through periods of extreme tension as well as physical duress without a flicker of panic and without tiring. You must be observant and able to give detailed written and oral reports without notes. And you must have an unblemished record. Even the smallest details of indiscretion will be learned by the C.I.A. in its intensive investigation of your background. The slightest weakness could be used by foreign agents against you.

However, these investigations can be in your favor. Once you have been hired by the C.I.A., the chances are very good that you will not be discharged. In terms of job security—if not personal security —the C.I.A. is a good place to work.

How might you get a job with the C.I.A.? The best way is to see your college recruiter. College seniors and graduate students in nearly all fields, but especially in international relations, economics, and political science, are needed. If you are a particularly bright student, you may already be under the watchful eye of the agency and will be approached by them. But if you have taken part in student marches protesting government policy, you had better look elsewhere for employment.

In its brochure entitled "Careers in Intelligence," the C.I.A. says:

"A prime need of the Central Intelligence Agency is for young men and women who have a liberal arts training—who have a strong sense of history, who are keenly aware of the forces of economics and politics—and who have substantial command of at least one foreign language. They must be well-adjusted young people with a strong inclination toward leadership. They must be willing to work anonymously. They must be able to see, think, and report clearly. They must be willing to accept responsibility and to serve in far places if need be.

"The worldwide search for truth often involves men and women trained in biology, geology, engineering, cartography, agriculture, even forestry. The C.I.A. often needs people whose specialties may seem superficially to be unrelated to the national security."

Although you would receive the usual government benefits of sick leave and retirement pensions, you would probably be paid less than by other employers. But if intelligence work intrigues you, you may apply either through your college placement office or by filling out an application form provided by:

> Central Intelligence Agency
> Office of Personnel
> 1016 16th Street, N.W.
> Washington, D.C.

United States Information Agency (U.S.I.A.)

No one who reads the daily newspapers can doubt the effectiveness of this agency in telling the United States story abroad. It is against the U.S.I.A. foreign centers and reading rooms that anti-American attacks have been directed.

The agency's Voice of America broadcasts 760 hours weekly by short wave in 36 languages to a worldwide audience of millions. An additional 14,000 hours weekly are broadcast overseas by 3,000 stations using material furnished by the U.S. Information Agency in 62 languages.

Agency films, with sound tracks in 52 languages, are available in 220 film libraries in 104 countries abroad. Nearly 600,000,000 people view these films every month.

Weekly 15-minute news and feature television shows are broadcast at peak viewing times in 48 cities in 18 Latin American countries.

Ten thousand words of commentaries, features, and background pieces are radio-teletyped daily to five world areas for distribution to local newspapers.

The U.S.I.A. maintains 182 libraries, 79 reading rooms, and 159 centers in 88 countries, and more than 300 exhibits are in constant worldwide circulation.

The agency publishes more than 18,000,000 copies of pamphlets in many languages, as well as four major magazines: *American Illustrated* (Russian edition) in 62,000 copies monthly; *American Illustrated* (Polish edition) in 33,000 copies monthly; *Al Hayat Fi America* (Arabic) in 30,000 copies monthly; and *Problems of Communism* (English and Spanish) in 30,000 copies every two months.

Overseas posts of the U.S.I.A. publish 65 other magazines and periodicals, as well as five cartoon features for newspapers in 87 countries.

In all of these mass communications media, the U.S.I.A. is performing its job of interpreting the United States and its policies and ideals abroad.

By its own admission, in a pamphlet entitled "Facts About U.S.I.A.," much of the agency's work is undramatic, "for in many areas apathy and suspicion are the enemies of understanding. Preconceptions about the United States abound, and some of them are distorted and unfavorable. Often success is measured in terms of good will gained, or simply in the removal of ill will. Many of the results of the U.S.I.A.'s work abroad are intangible; they are long-term, quiet, and usually unreported."

Career opportunities with the U.S.I.A. usually fall into two categories: informational and cultural.

If you are interested in the informational aspects, you must have training or experience in one or more of the communications media.

For an appointment in cultural affairs, you must have experience in teaching or research, a working knowledge of one of the creative arts, or experience in some phase of international cultural relations.

If you have experience in administration, library work, or teaching, you might work in one of the agency's bi-national centers.

For any job with the U.S.I.A., a good working knowledge of a foreign language and an ability to learn languages is required. You must also be able to convey information convincingly and tactfully, orally and in writing, and have a solid background in American foreign policy and international relations as well as United States history, political science, and economics.

It should go without saying that you must be willing to serve at any post in any country.

The foreign service of the United States Information Agency is set up much like the diplomatic corps. It comprises members of the career reserve corps and a limited reserve corps, which is made up of people who wish to serve a maximum of five years. In addition, the agency has a junior reserve officer corps.

To qualify for the junior career reserve officer corps, you must be between twenty-one and thirty-one years of age, an American citizen for at least ten years, and meet rigid physical requirements. The agency normally does not employ spouses of agency employees, married women, or women with dependents.

The written and oral examinations for the U.S.I.A. are identical with those for the diplomatic corps except that you must choose to be examined under Option A in Part 4 of the test, dealing with history, government, social sciences, and public affairs.

If you have experience in broadcasting and are interested in the Voice of America's career intern program in broadcasting, you would be required to take a voicing-writing test. This test consists of writing a 50- to 60-line commentary on a speech made by President Johnson and recording your commentary on tape. If you speak a foreign language you would write and record a three-minute commentary on the speech in that language. You would also be required to write an original 60-line script on "Automation and the Future," and prepare a five-minute newscast using a single edition of a metropolitan newspaper.

Similar internship programs are available in management and in other phases of the information agency.

Applicants for the U.S.I.A.'s foreign service junior training center program should write to:

Joint Board of Examiners
United States Information Agency
Washington, D.C. 20547

Applicants between the ages of thirty-one and fifty-four should write to:

Personnel Services Staff
United States Information Agency
Washington, D.C. 20547

Peace Corps

Much has been written about the Peace Corps volunteers and the exciting work they are doing all over the world.

Volunteers range in age from eighteen to seventy-two and serve in Latin America, Africa, the Caribbean, and the Near and Far East. Many of them are teachers—of all subjects at all levels. Demand is heavy for teachers of science and mathematics. Second in demand are people with agricultural and farm backgrounds. Carpenters, bricklayers, nurses, doctors, well-drillers, home economists are needed. The list is endless.

You may apply for the Peace Corps by filling out a questionnaire, which is available at most Post Offices, from the national headquarters in Washington, or from your Congressman.

You may request an area in which you would like to serve, and you may ask to serve with another person. (Husband-and-wife teams are often sent out.) The corps will honor your request if possible.

When you have been accepted by the Peace Corps, you will begin three months of intensive study, sometimes running to 60 hours a week. After this phase is completed, you will be sent to one of three training sites, where language study is intensified, field experience is gained, and physical conditioning programs are completed.

The usual term of service is two years, including training, and the pay is low. In addition to housing and food during training, volunteers receive two dollars a day expense money. In the field they receive a living allowance for housing, food, and incidental expenses, but only enough to allow them to live at the level of the people with whom they work.

Volunteers also receive a readjustment allowance of $75 a month for each month of service, including training. While overseas, they receive 45 days of leave time and $7.50 a day during it, but they may not return to the United States except in cases of family emergency. They are encouraged to tour the country in which they work and may get permission to travel to a nearby country.

Why might you want to work with the Peace Corps? The nature of the corps is such that it attracts people dedicated to helping.

And what happens when you get home?

President John F. Kennedy, addressing a group of outgoing volunteers, said:

"I hope that when you get back we can persuade you to come and serve in the United States government in other areas, particularly foreign service. I hope you will regard this as the first installment in a long life of service in the most exciting career in the most exciting time."

Graduates of the Peace Corps program are also needed in industry. Thomas J. Watson, Jr., president of International Business Machines, said:

"It seems clear to me that members of the Peace Corps will be particularly employable when they complete their tours of duty. They will have demonstrated their ability to take on tough jobs under extremely difficult circumstances and to follow them through to their completion. There are never enough people of this kind available for any enterprise."

If you are an American citizen, are at least eighteen years old, are available to serve two years, and, if married, have no dependents under eighteen, you may apply by submitting a questionnaire or writing to:

> Peace Corps
> Washington, D.C. 20525
> Attention: Office of Public Affairs

Civil Service

Since we have mentioned Civil Service frequently and since it is so often a vital part of employment with the United States government, perhaps we should discuss briefly how you acquire "Civil Service status."

There are six steps to a job in competitive Civil Service.

1. *Find out about examinations.* Check with the Post Office, college placement office, or Civil Service Commission for the latest examination announcement for your field of interest, which will list the experience and/or education required for a given job.

2. *Fill out the application forms* specified in the announcement and mail them before the deadline to the designated address.

3. *Take the test* if one is required. You may indicate where you would like to take the test, and you will be notified of the exact location and date. If a test is not required, you will be rated on experience and education. It is important that you include on your application form all pertinent facts about your education and experience.

4. *Wait for the test results.* You must make a passing score of at least 70 points. You will be notified whether you have received an "eligible" or "ineligible" rating, and the score you received. If you are eligible, your name will be entered on the list in order of rank determined by your score on the test.

5. You may be asked to come in for an *interview.* Each hiring official has a choice from among the top three eligibles for each job to be filled. If you are not selected, your name will be returned to the eligible list for consideration when other vacancies occur.

6. *Consider your chances of employment.* This will depend on how well you scored in the examination and how fast vacancies occur. Remember that if you specify geographic locations for employment and a salary or grade you are willing to accept, you are not just indicating a preference. You will be considered only for jobs in the area and at the salary or grade you indicated. However, no matter what minimum salary or grade level you set, you will be rated for the highest level for which you can qualify.

Civil Service Regional Offices

For more information regarding Civil Service jobs, write to:

Director, —————— Region, U.S. Civil Service Commission. States included in the various regions are as follows:

Alabama, Florida, Georgia, Mississippi, North and South Carolina, Tennessee, Puerto Rico, Virgin Islands—Atlanta Region, 240 Peachtree Street, Atlanta, Georgia.

Connecticut, Maine, Massachusetts, New Hampshire, Rhode Island, Vermont—Boston Region, Post Office and Courthouse Building, Boston, Massachusetts 02109.

Illinois, Indiana, Kentucky, Michigan, Ohio, Wisconsin—Chicago Region, Main Post Office Building, Chicago, Illinois 60607.

Arkansas, Louisiana, Oklahoma, Texas—Dallas Region, 1114 Commerce Street, Dallas, Texas 75202.

Arizona, Colorado, New Mexico, Utah, Wyoming—Denver Region, Building 41, Denver Federal Center, Denver, Colorado 80225.

Delaware, Maryland, Pennsylvania, Virginia, West Virginia—Philadelphia Region, Customhouse, 2nd and Chestnut Streets, Philadelphia, Pennsylvania 19106.

New Jersey, New York—New York Region, News Building, 220 East 42nd Street, New York, N.Y. 10017.

California, Hawaii, Nevada—San Francisco Region, 128 Appraisers Building, 630 Sansome Street, San Francisco, California 94111.

Alaska, Idaho, Montana, Oregon, Washington—Seattle Region, 302 Federal Office Building, First Avenue and Madison Street, Seattle, Washington 98104.

Iowa, Kansas, Minnesota, Missouri, Nebraska, North and South Dakota—St. Louis Region, Federal Building, 1520 Market Street, St. Louis, Missouri 63103.

CHAPTER XII

How Manpower Inc. Can Help You Get a Job Abroad

If your idea of overseas travel is not hopping from one big city to another with just enough time to take a quick look at the major sights, perhaps Manpower Inc. can help you. If you would like an extended visit to England, and if you have secretarial skills, you can qualify for Manpower's work-travel program.

Although Manpower will not provide your transportation overseas, it can assure sufficient income once you arrive to pay for food, lodging, and utilities, with enough left over to pay for incidentals during your stay.

Manpower Inc. is the world's largest employer of men and women who want to work on a part-time or temporary basis. Its services are used by business firms throughout the world when they have too much work for their own personnel to handle. For example, when a typist goes on vacation, a company will call Manpower to fill in until she returns. Or, when there is a backlog of typing, reports to be completed by a deadline, or rush work to get out, Manpower employees are called upon to help meet the emergency.

In addition to over four hundred offices in the United States and Canada, Manpower has over one hundred overseas offices—a total of 536 offices in thirty-four countries on six continents.

As I have pointed out earlier, government restrictions in many countries prohibit employment of nonnationals. This means, in effect, that even though we have Manpower offices all over the world, each of our foreign offices must abide by the immigration rules set forth by its own government.

At the present time, foreign immigration rules have prevented our organization from developing the type of overseas work-travel program we would like to have. When our plan was set up originally, we were able to send qualified applicants to Manpower offices in four different countries; unfortunately, this is no longer the case.

We do have an excellent work-travel arrangement with our Manpower offices in the United Kingdom, so if it is your desire to get acquainted with fascinating London or any of the other cities in England where there is a Manpower office, we would welcome an inquiry from you. If you wish detailed information, address your inquiry to Manpower's home office, 820 N. Plankinton Ave., Milwaukee, Wis. 53203.

There are four main requirements to qualify for Manpower's overseas work-travel program:

1. You must be an experienced female secretary, able to take shorthand at 120 words per minute and type 60 to 65 words per minute.
2. You must be between the ages of twenty-one and fifty-four.
3. You must be willing to work for two consecutive months for Manpower Inc. in the London area.
4. In addition to being adaptable and skilled, you must be adventurous and able to take minor difficulties in stride.

If you meet these qualifications and can pay for your transportation, you might well be on your way to a self-supported tour.

Let us talk briefly about England, the kind of work you might do there for Manpower, and the government regulations that would affect your work.

In England, Manpower now has twenty offices, but most of the opportunities for employment are in London. Work permits for Americans are available only from April 1 to October 30, and the job skills most in demand are stenographic, typing, dictaphone, and general secretarial. There is very little opportunity for other types of office work.

Governmental regulations specify that aliens entering to work in England must either have a return ticket or be able to prove that they have sufficient funds to purchase a ticket home.

Ann Shteir, who worked for Manpower Inc. in London, warns anyone planning on working in England to familiarize herself with British spelling. "But," she adds philosophically, "such preparation can be easily accomplished by one day of errors."

She also advises against being shy. You are as interesting to the others as they are to you.

The Manpower office in London can certainly offer summer jobs to American girls. The office advises that you should be receptive and tolerant of the English reserve, "which is not as acute as some would believe, as more and more the friendly American influence is creeping in."

Perhaps Manpower Inc. can be of help to you in another way, too. If you are already in another country and have a working visa, and if you wish to work for Manpower Inc., you may apply at one of the following offices:

AFRICA
Nigeria, Lagos
South Africa, Durban, Natal
South Africa, Johannesburg

ASIA
B.C.C., Hong Kong
Japan, Tokyo
Philippines, Manila
Singapore, Singapore
Taiwan, Taipei
Thailand, Bangkok

AUSTRALIA
Adelaide
Brisbane
Melbourne
Perth
Sydney

CANADA
Belleville, Ont.
Brockville, Ont.
Calgary, Alta.
Edmonton, Alta.
Guelph, Ont.

Halifax, N. S.
Hamilton, Ont.
Kingston, Ont.
Kitchener, Ont.
London, Ont.
Montreal, Que.
Niagara Falls, Ont.
Ottawa, Ont.
Owen Sound, Ont.
Quebec City, Que.
Regina, Sask.
St. Catherine's, Ont.
Saskatoon, Sask.
Toronto, Ont.
    Don Mills-Scarboro, Ont.
    Weston, Ont.
Vancouver, B. C.
Windsor, Ont.
Winnipeg, Man.

EUROPE

Belgium
Antwerp
Baudour-Lez-Mons
Brussels
Eupen

Liége
Verviers

Denmark
Aarhus
Copenhagen
Odense

England
Birmingham
Blackburn
Bolton
Brighton
Bristol
Fareham
Leeds

London Metropolitan Area
Fleet Street, E.C.4.
Hammersmith, W.6.
Jermyn Street, S.W.1.
Marylebone High Street, W.1.
Notting Hill Gate, W.11.
Walworth Road, S.E. 17.
Manchester
Middlesbrough
Portsmouth
Preston
Reading
Southampton
Stoke-on-Trent

France
Bordeaux
Grenoble
Lille
Lyons
Marseilles
Metz

Mulhouse
Paris
Roubaix

Germany
Düsseldorf
Frankfurt

Greece, Athens

Norway, Oslo

Portugal
Lisbon
Porto

Switzerland
Basel
Geneva
Lausanne
Zurich

Turkey
Ankara
Istanbul

MEXICO
Mexico City

LATIN AMERICA

Argentina, Buenos Aires

Brazil
Rio de Janeiro
São Paulo
Santo Andre

Chile
Concepción
Santiago

Colombia
Bogotá

Cali
Medellín
Panama, Panama City
Paraguay, Asunción
Peru, Lima

THE WEST INDIES

Jamaica, Kingston

Bahamas, Nassau

Puerto Rico, Santurce

CHAPTER XIII

Seventeen Fields That Offer Some Opportunities for Working Abroad

In earlier chapters we have talked in general terms—and usually in other contexts—about where and at what you might work abroad. But there are some kinds of work and some general fields of employment that can involve travel.

What follows is a listing—in alphabetical order for your convenience —of seventeen of these fields. Many of them, although not generally related in this country, are closely connected in overseas operations. An oil firm, for example, would employ nurses and teachers in its overseas hospitals and schools. A banking firm might have an overseas public relations staff. You will find separate listings for nurses (under medicine), teaching, and advertising and public relations.

At the end of the alphabetical listing is a short section on ways you might travel with pay by using your own ingenuity.

Advertising and Public Relations

If you have visited any of the major foreign cities, you were probably struck by the familiar billboards advertising American-made products—Liggett and Myers cigarettes, Coca-Cola, Singer sewing machines, Procter and Gamble products. (A recent traveler to Amman, Jordan, was amazed at the hundreds of shiny new Plymouths on the main thoroughfares.)

Obviously, a lot of advertising men must be employed abroad. How are your chances? Regrettably, not very good. You must be at least bilingual, and this means fluent in another language, especially in its idiomatic forms.

You might work for an American advertising agency abroad, and some Americans do. Generally, though, they are people with many years of experience at home, usually with the New York-based agencies. As in other industries, advertising agencies turn their foreign operations over to nationals who have a built-in familiarity not only with the language but also with customs, selling, and consumer research. Even motivational research is becoming a major factor in overseas advertising.

Your best opportunities in advertising and public relations are with American firms other than agencies. Construction, oil, mining, and rubber firms employ men in advertising overseas, as do many other large firms.

You may inquire about European advertising agencies by writing to:

E. A. A. A.
Dufourstrasse, 155
Zurich, Switzerland

Banking and Finance

Many American banks have overseas branches, but most of the personnel are nationals. Many years of experience and a detailed knowledge of international finance are basic requirements in this field. Most of the Americans employed abroad in banking and finance are experts in international finance who are in top executive positions.

There are, of course, traineeship programs under which students in economics and commerce work abroad for two- to six-month periods (see Chapter XIV). Two girls under such a program in Israel found themselves pressed into service one summer when the Bank Leumi was faced with a problem. Six hundred Baptist pilgrims were scheduled to cross through the Mandelbaum gate, the only opening between Jordan and Israel, on a Saturday, which is the Jewish Sabbath. Since none of the bank's regular employees could work on that day, these girls, both Roman Catholic, volunteered their services and, after a crash training program in foreign currency exchange, handled the visitors with all the aplomb of seasoned veterans.

Construction

Since jobs in construction vary almost daily with the awarding of new contracts, it is impossible to list specific openings. But American "know-how" is at a premium all over the world for large-scale construction. Americans are helping to build airfields, highways, dams, military bases, and railroads. Electricians, surveyors, engineers of all kinds, architects, equipment operators, mechanics, welders, and truck drivers can all be used on overseas projects.

Working for a private construction firm can net you high earnings and an equally high standard of living abroad. And since you are usually required to sign a contract for two years, you can often qualify for total exemption from U.S. income tax.

There are disadvantages, however. It is not often possible for your family to accompany you—at least, not right away. Then, of course, there may be the discomforts of climate. Much construction work is being done by American companies in very hot climates accompanied either by a total lack of rainfall or by constant rain.

Since no general listing of jobs is available, probably your best bet would be to try one or more of the agencies that specialize in overseas employment. The following are all in New York City.

Archer Personnel Agency, Inc.—301 Madison Avenue
Foreign Language Bureau—132 Nassau Street
Garon-Walker—45 West 45th Street
Maude Lennox Personnel Service, Inc.—630 Fifth Avenue
Leland F. Perkins, Inc.—420 Lexington Avenue
Universal Technical Agency—217 Broadway
Elizabeth Ewers—150 Nassau Street

You might check the classified sections of telephone directories in the major cities for contracting firms and send letters of application and résumés to those that seem most likely to have overseas contracts.

The business news pages of the major newspapers, especially the New York *Times,* might provide job leads in news stories about contracts awarded. The "Foreign Projects Newsletter" of which we spoke earlier also might be a good source.

Other information on current construction projects is obtainable by writing:

Transportation and Utilities Staff
Office of Economic Affairs
Bureau of Foreign Commerce
U.S. Department of Commerce
Washington, D.C.

Home Economics

The broad employment opportunities for the home economist in this country are virtually unknown abroad. A woman may become a teacher of domestic science abroad, but the field of adult education in a university extension division is totally unexplored.

A foreign counterpart of our home economist might work for a commercial firm, but always in a selling capacity. If she were working in child welfare, her field would be sociology. Interior decorating is a man's field abroad, but women are employed in the textile industry in design and research.

If you would like to work abroad as a home economist, you may write for additional information:

American Home Economics Association
1600 20th Street, N.W.
Washington, D.C. 20009

Library Work

In outposts all over the world, American librarians work in U.S. Information Agency libraries, maintaining reading rooms, selling specially printed low-cost paperbacks about American life, and keeping track of the hundreds of films and tape recordings circulated throughout the free world.

For more information about the program, write to:

Director of Personnel
United States Information Agency
Department of State
Washington, D.C.

Medicine

Nursing is one of the fields in which a well-paid job is most readily available for girls. Nurses are needed everywhere.

If you want to use your nursing skills to provide you with travel, you may choose from a variety of jobs. You could be a commissioned officer in the Army Nurse Corps, where after nine weeks of basic training and six months in an Army hospital in the United States, you might be sent to Japan, Alaska, Hawaii, or anywhere else the Army has a hospital. You must be a registered professional nurse, a graduate of a school of nursing acceptable to the Surgeon General, and between twenty-one and forty-four years of age. If assigned overseas, you would be expected to serve a minimum of two years. You can get information from the nearest Army recruiting center.

You can qualify as a flight nurse in the Air Force if you are under thirty-six, are a graduate of an acceptable nursing school, and can pass the required physical examination. You would spend three weeks in basic training and six months in an Air Force hospital before being sent overseas. Flight training is given at Gunter Air Force Base, Alabama. You can get more information from:

Surgeon General
U.S. Air Force
Washington, D.C.

Navy nurses must spend eighteen months in the United States before being sent overseas. You can get information from the nearest Navy recruiting office or from:

Bureau of Medicine and Surgery
U.S. Navy
Washington, D.C.

You can work for the government in public health nursing as a civilian, sent to another country by the Federal Security Agency. You can also work in the Panama Canal Zone. Public health experience is not required, but you must have at least one year of practical experience. You can inquire about possible vacancies by writing:

Chief of Office
Panama Canal Company
411 10th Street, N.W.
Washington, D.C.

The United States Foreign Service also employs nurses, who are usually stationed at posts where medical facilities are below standard and where the health of staff or local employees may be a problem.

As a Foreign Service nurse you would develop and administer medical and health programs for embassy personnel, instruct newly arrived personnel on hygiene and disease prevention, immunize employees, be on call twenty-four hours a day to treat illness and injuries, and regularly visit employees and their dependents at home and in the hospital to be sure that they were getting adequate care.

You would be stationed at any of 300 posts in 100 countries and would earn $6,225 plus appropriate allowances. As a member of the Foreign Service Staff Corps, you would also receive leave time and other benefits.

To qualify, you must be single, at least twenty-five years of age, and a citizen of the United States for five years. You must be a graduate registered nurse, and preference is given to nurses who have a B.S. degree in nursing and at least one year of experience in public health or industrial nursing. Graduates of accredited schools of nursing with two years of experience, at least one of which must be in the above fields, will also be considered. For more information, write:

> Employment Division
> Department of State
> Washington, D.C.

The most obvious openings for nurses abroad are with the mission boards of the several religious organizations. The pay is comparatively low, the terms of service are usually longer than with other jobs, and usually the posts are far from the major European cities. But if you would like to use your nursing skills helping people who really need it, and if you are willing to live on $80 to $200 a month comfortably, but not in luxury, then missionary nursing may be for you.

Contact your church's mission board or write to:

> Division of Foreign Missions
> National Council of Churches
> 475 Riverside Drive
> New York, N.Y.

Similar low-in-pay but rich-in-satisfaction jobs are available for both doctors and nurses in such organizations as MEDICO and the Thomas Dooley Foundation in San Francisco. The cry for medical help all over the world is constant, and more than 2,000 American doctors already are working abroad. Sometimes they work in well-equipped hospitals with everything a physician and surgeon might require. More often, however, their hospitals are built in the depths of the jungle or in a truly depressed area where the need is evident.

Modeling

In the United States a model need only be sufficiently attractive and trained in the grooming and the proper stance to show clothes. You might find a job as a photographer's model in New York or doing "informal modeling" in a department store. You might even model on television, or be seen at the local auto show prettying up the newest models.

But jobs like these are virtually unknown abroad. This is not to say that the high fashion houses in Paris do not hire non-French girls. Some of the best-known and highest-paid models are girls from outside of France, but they are exceptional girls with exceptional qualifications.

Mining

United States firms have mining operations all over the world, and if this is your field in any of its many facets, you can probably get a job abroad. What we have said about construction is generally true for mining.

To apply for a job, it is wise to check the classified section of the New York telephone directory, and send letters and résumés to the companies that look most promising. The business pages of the New York *Times,* particularly the Sunday edition, can also be helpful.

Because mining operations usually hire nationals as laborers, there are no jobs for the unskilled in foreign mines. There are jobs, however, for mine foremen, engineers, geologists, metallurgists, and chemists.

Newspapers

The public's picture of a newspaperman overseas is a romantic one of a hard-fisted reporter who covers his international beat without batting an eyelash. Unhappily the picture is far from reality.

There are jobs for Americans on some of the English-language dailies found in many of the major cities of the world, but be forewarned. These papers are not waiting breathlessly for the new journalism graduate to come to clean up their page make-up and turn the paper into a gleaming copy of the current American prize-winners. In too many cases, they are happy with their typographical errors and sometimes vague copy. Generally they are inferior to the national papers, some of which enjoy the prestige of being close to the government.

A notable exception is the *International Herald Tribune,* a highly regarded newspaper, which uses Americans only.

The major radio and TV networks staff their news departments from their home offices.

The Army's *Stars and Stripes* employs civilian personnel abroad wherever the paper is published.

Every newspaperman is familiar with the money to be made as a "stringer," who files stories from his area directed to the specific audience of the publication for which he works. Many trade publications —McGraw-Hill publishes many of them in diverse fields—as well as major American newspapers employ stringers, and this might be a way for you to pick up some of your travel expenses.

In nearly every issue, *Editor and Publisher* runs at least one classified advertisement to this effect:

"Your man in Paris for $50 a week. Will file stories, features, and your assignments. Fluent French; 15 years abroad."

If you are a member of the Overseas Press Club, check into its no-charge placement service.

Office Work

We have said a great deal about how you can go abroad as a secretary, either for the government or for private industry, but openings for office help are also available in some of the many service agencies operating abroad.

The American Red Cross is a typical example. Apart from women workers in recreation, the Red Cross hires only stenographers directly for overseas work.

You must be between twenty-three and thirty-five years of age, in good health, and a citizen of the United States, and must have at least a year's experience in office work and a knowledge of typing, shorthand, and office procedures.

Stenographers and recreation workers are usually sent directly overseas for a two-year period, then returned to the United States for duty.

As in work for the armed forces, Red Cross workers must be willing to serve wherever sent, usually in the offices of administrative officers or field directors in a military hospital.

The Red Cross continues its statement of qualifications:

"The applicant should be well-groomed and attractive, friendly but impersonal in her attitude toward men, and mature in judgment. She should possess a sense of humor, sincerity of purpose, resourcefulness, and imagination. She should have the ability to recognize and adhere to military etiquette and regulations, to adjust to uncertain assignments and changing conditions, to win the respect of those with whom she comes into contact, and to work as a member of a group."

If you think you might qualify, write for further information to:

Personnel Services
American Red Cross
18th & D Streets, N.W.
Washington, D.C.

Similar jobs abroad may be had with other service agencies, all of which need secretarial help.

Again, there are secretarial jobs with the government (see Chapter XI) and with Manpower, Inc. (see Chapter XII).

Oil

The Middle East, Latin America, and the northwestern part of Canada are the new sites for a rapidly expanding oil industry, although, of course, there are other oil operations in other parts of the world.

Most of the large American oil companies have drilling and refinery operations abroad, the best now being Aramco (Arabian American Oil Company) in Saudi Arabia. Aramco hires highly skilled employees in technical fields as well as American teachers, nurses, and clerical help. The address of the Personnel Office in New York is 505 Park Avenue.

Experts in petroleum are also sent by Standard Oil of New Jersey, which operates primarily in South America. The unskilled work is done by nationals.

Sinclair Oil Company fills most of its positions in Venezuela and Ethiopia from within the organization. Pay is high, but housing for dependents is scarce.

Other oil companies employing Americans overseas are: Atlantic Refining Company, Creole Petroleum Corp., Gulf Oil Corp., International Petroleum Corp., Socony Mobil Oil Company, California Texas Oil Corp., and the Texas Company.

Most of the jobs in refineries are in Latin America. A list of those currently operating can be had from the commercial attachés of the Latin American embassies and from the Pan American Union in Washington.

Personnel

As you might expect, someone has to screen and hire those prospective employees abroad. But as we have pointed out, most of the hiring is done in this country for overseas positions.

Personnel work for foreign firms is done by nationals who are not only fluent in the language, but are familiar with the labor market and with the requirements and job demands of prospective employers. Rarely, if ever, is an American employed in the personnel division of a foreign firm.

Radio and Television

If you are an American citizen, have a good working knowledge of a foreign language, have a recent college degree in communications, journalism, foreign affairs, government, foreign languages, and area studies, and have a voice suitable for broadcasting, you may find a career with the Voice of America, under the jurisdiction of the United States Information Agency (see Chapter XI). The requirements for international broadcasters fall into six types:

1. The ability to write competently in English and/or a foreign language.
2. The ability to acquire information about different subjects and to prepare the information in a style suitable to radio.
3. The ability to understand and apply a knowledge of the history, customs, and thinking of the American people and United States foreign policy to radio programming.
4. A similar knowledge of the culture, mores, and thinking of the audience and the ability to adapt programming in a style appropriate to the audience.

5. A speaking voice suitable for international broadcasting in English or in the language of the area of broadcast reception.
6. A strong interest in international broadcasting.

Skilled Craftsmen

We have covered many of the jobs that are available to skilled craftsmen overseas, but for review, here are some of your prospective employers abroad.

1. The private company in your field. Again, try the classified section of the telephone directory or the Sunday edition of the New York *Times*.
2. A private company in the area in which you would like to work. Australia and New Zealand are hoping that skilled craftsmen will immigrate.
3. The government, as a civilian employee at one of the hundreds of military bases around the world. (Of course, you *could* join the Army and see the world as a skilled craftsman. The pay is low, but you would gain additional training in the Army, Navy, or Air Force.)
4. The voluntary organizations, including the Peace Corps.

Working for an American firm abroad might net you a real bank balance when you get home. Not only is the pay generally good, but there is plenty of overtime. Much of the work is being done in what are termed hardship posts and carries an extra allowance for that as well as a separation allowance if you are married.

You may be sure you will be well screened before an American company sends you abroad. Your health as well as your stability must be excellent. You must be easy to get along with and have great patience. You may well find yourself working with illiterates whose standard of work is considerably lower than at home.

You must be a journeyman in your trade with at least four years of experience. While you are looking for work abroad, check with your union. They often get word of jobs for journeymen overseas.

Sports and Recreation

We have already mentioned the requirements for recreation specialists with the American Red Cross, which hires people directly for overseas posts.

A girl college graduate who is over twenty-one years of age may find a job as a recreation specialist with the Army. This could be a plush civilian job, working in servicemen's clubs all over the world and being paid $4,690 a year.

The State Department's cultural affairs division employs coaches, and coaches can teach in American overseas schools. Men can also work for the Department of Defense as coaches both in and out of the armed service. And again, the Peace Corps can use you.

Teaching

Although many men are employed as teachers, most of the teachers sent overseas are women.

Since we shall deal with higher education in the next chapter, we shall confine our discussion for the time being to the teaching of children abroad. (Of course, you might get a job as an untrained teacher of English to people of all ages; many Americans abroad are doing just that.)

Suppose you are a second-grade teacher in an American school and that your summer travel (which is nearly compulsory for teachers under the terms of their contracts) has whetted your appetite for travel abroad.

With the nationwide teacher shortage, you could be fairly certain of getting another job on your return. You might investigate teaching jobs abroad. Most such jobs might be a great deal like your job at home, since most teachers working abroad teach in schools for American children, whether in the military or in private industry. The appeal of teaching overseas would probably lie in your proximity to new and exciting sights that you could explore in your off-hours.

The government employs teachers in military dependents' schools (see Chapter XI), and large American companies have similar jobs. Private elementary and secondary schools are operated by nationals to meet the needs of their children, and churches operate schools. Although church organizations and private firms often do their own recruiting, you can get information about jobs in Latin America in American-sponsored bi-national schools, from:

Inter-American Schools Service
1785 Massachusetts Avenue
Washington, D.C.

A free booklet entitled "Teaching Opportunities in Latin America for U.S. Citizens" is available from:

Division of Education
Pan American Union
19th and Constitution Avenue, N.W.
Washington, D.C.

Teachers can work overseas in many other ways, among them the United States Teacher Exchange program (the Fulbright Act), under which you might qualify for a leave of absence from your school to teach abroad, while a foreign teacher worked in your place. Transportation is provided for a teacher, but not for dependents. Since, as a government employee, your income would be taxable in the United States, you might receive an additional grant of $1,000 to cover taxes. If you would like to inquire about taking part in a teacher exchange program, write:

Teacher Exchange Section
Division of International Education
Office of Education
Department of Health, Education, and Welfare
Washington, D.C.

The French government awards about 40 teaching assistantships annually to teachers, to conduct classes in English conversation in French secondary schools. Preference is given to those who have not had a chance to study abroad and to candidates who intend to teach French.

To qualify, you must be single, hold a bachelor's degree, be under thirty years of age, and an American citizen. You must have a good working knowledge of French and will be required to submit a recording of your spoken French and English.

For further information, write:

The Counseling Division, Institute of International Education
809 United Nations Plaza
New York, New York 10017

Candidates must be prepared to pay their own travel expenses, but may apply for one of the U.S. Government Travel-Only grants from the same address. The deadline for applying for these grants is February 1.

A similar opportunity awaits you in towns and small cities throughout Germany, where you would teach English conversation and reading, rather than give full language instruction.

To qualify for the German teaching assistantships, you must have at least a bachelor's degree in German, English, history, political science, or education. You must be single, between twenty-one and thirty years of age, and a U.S. citizen.

Applications must be submitted to the German Embassy or a German consulate. You will then have a personal interview with the cultural attaché or his assistant.

You may get further information and application forms from:

Pedagogischer Austauschdienst
Bonn, Königstrasse 61, Germany

If you would like to teach in Great Britain or Northern Ireland, you can apply directly to the governing bodies of the schools. For information, write:

British Information Services
845 Third Avenue
New York, New York 10022

In order to teach in schools supported by public money in the United Kingdom, you must meet certain teacher qualifications. This is not necessary in private schools, but the standards are usually the same, if not higher.

Vacancies in schools are usually advertised in British educational papers, such as the *Times Educational Supplement, The Teacher,* and *Education.* If you are in the New York area, you may see these in the library at the British Information Agency. Large public libraries and university libraries also often have them on file.

Vacancies for teaching positions are often filled through scholastic agencies. The largest ones are:

Truman and Knightly, Ltd.
91–93 Baker Street
London, W.1

Gabbitas-Thring Educational Trust
6 Sackville Street
London, W.1

J. and J. Paton, Ltd.
Ormond House
63 Queen Victoria Street
London, E.C.4

These, of course, are commercial agencies and charge a fee for their services.

New Zealand has vacancies for qualified teachers of mathematics, general science, English/social studies, and commercial subjects. Most vacancies are in schools in country, provincial, and recently developed housing areas.

For raises in salary at both the high-school and elementary level, you must have spent at least three years in "country service," outside the main centers of population, although exceptions are sometimes made for people with wide trade or teaching experience. Complete exemption from "country service" is granted to elementary teachers who are over thirty and to high-school teachers who are over thirty-two.

Travel

At the outset, it would seem that the easiest way to travel and get paid for it is to work for an agency or company engaged in the business of traveling.

Steamship lines and freighters ply the oceans by the hundreds, with sometimes hundreds of people employed on each ship. What are your chances of visits to strange and fascinating ports as a part of the ship's crew?

You must have seaman's papers (a U.S. Coast Guard Certificate) before you can work anywhere at any job on board ship. You can get these papers by applying at the Marine Inspection Service offices in the major port cities. You need be only seventeen to apply, but the Coast Guard warns that few new papers are being issued because of severe unemployment.

If you have money to get you through the waiting period, you might go to one of the port cities—the Gulf ports are usually better bets than cities on the East or West Coast—until a job turns up.

Several jobs on board ship are available even to the inexperienced. Men might work as an ordinary seaman on the deck of an American ship (or deck boy on a foreign line), as a wiper in the engine room, or as a utilityman or messman in the steward's department. You might also be employed as a bellboy, porter, elevator operator, or library steward.

A woman might get a job as a social director on one of the ten American lines that employ them. A social director, man or woman, is responsible for planning parties and dances, bridge tournaments, games, and contests, and serves as master of ceremonies, host, and matchmaker. Languages are absolutely required.

You can travel with an *airline* as a pilot or stewardess if you meet the qualifications.

To be a pilot for Pan American Airlines, you must be twenty to twenty-seven years of age at the time you are hired and must have at least two years of college. You must be a citizen of the United States and able to obtain a passport. Your military service must be completed and you must have an F.A.A. commercial license and instrument rating as well as a minimum of 500 hours single- or multi-engine flying time.

Formerly it was a requirement that all stewardesses flying overseas be registered nurses and speak at least one other language. With the increase in air travel, the nursing requirement was dropped, though the language requirement is still in effect with some lines.

Stewardesses may draw overseas flights with some lines strictly on a seniority basis; currently it takes roughly two to two and a half years for a stewardess to gain enough seniority with Northwest-Orient Airlines to draw one of their overseas schedules.

For information about flying jobs with the major airlines, write to the following addresses:

American Airlines—633 Third Avenue, New York, N.Y.
Continental Airlines, Inc.—Stapleton Airfield, Denver, Colorado.
Delta Airlines, Inc.—Municipal Airport, Atlanta, Georgia.

Eastern Airlines, Inc.—10 Rockefeller Plaza, New York, N.Y. 10017.

Northwest Orient Airlines—Minneapolis, Minnesota.

Pan American World Airways System, Inc.—135 East 42nd Street, New York, N.Y.

United Airlines—O'Hare International Airport, Box 8800, Chicago, Illinois.

Newspapers in the major cities carry advertisements announcing interviews for stewardesses. Usually two years of college or work experience is required.

If you are an experienced traveler, have spent a lot of time in another country, and are familiar with its attractions, you might become a *tour director* or manager. You must like to be with people and be concerned about their welfare; you must be able to cope with petty problems and the uncertainties of a mixed group of strangers in strange surroundings, and you must be able to make them glad that they have come.

There are many ways in which you might become a tour leader without much travel experience. Many airlines will pay your transportation and sometimes your expenses abroad, if you arrange a tour of your friends and your friends' friends. To qualify, you must have a minimum of 15 people. A travel agency will book your hotels and restaurants, if you wish. You then have only to contact a local guide and you find yourself abroad with a minimum of expense.

Much publicity has been given recently to the U.S. Travel Service. The U.S.T.S. has offices in London, Paris, Rome, Frankfurt, Sydney, Tokyo, Mexico City, and Bogotá for the express purpose of promoting travel in the United States.

The agency, a part of the Department of Commerce, operates on a very small budget, however, and employs only about 50 people, including nationals in its overseas offices. You could apply and put your name on the waiting list, but don't expect to be called for a few years.

You can always go abroad and take your chances on picking up small tours of Americans on your own. For example, you might invest in a car or small bus and set yourself up in business as a guide for short jaunts. This has been done successfully.

One American in Paris has established a good business based on tours for children only, taking them to see the things that interest them and freeing the parents for a day at the Louvre or other adult activities.

At last report, this was the only such service available in Europe. Why not set up a similar service in Rome or London?

American Ingenuity

As hackneyed as the phrase may sound, "American ingenuity" is widely recognized, and there is no reason why you can't use yours to pay your way abroad or at least defray part of your expenses.

The following suggestions have already been done, and perhaps the market has reached saturation point. But they might start you thinking about talents you have to help you get abroad.

Do you have writing skills? We have already mentioned some of the more conventional ways a writer abroad can make money.

One reporter, unable to crack the major news agencies abroad, set up his own agency in Brussels and is doing well at it. If you are an established writer and employed by an American newspaper, perhaps you could sell your paper on sending you abroad to cover something in your specialty.

A business news writer was sent abroad to cover the Common Market and file a series of stories. The paper paid his expenses, and he picked up enough information on the side to write a free-lance story for a major magazine.

You might go over on your own money, and on your return sell stories to publications to help you pay for your next trip. Bear in mind, though, that you must have something to write besides "The Impressions of an American in Paris."

One writer on her return from Israel wrote her reactions as a Christian and sold the articles to Jewish publications.

You might also give travel lectures, but you must know your subject. If you have pictures to show, know what they are. One lecturer who tried to show 1,000 slides in an hour told his audience that "This is where some guy who wrote a symphony, I think, lived." It was the home of Giuseppe Verdi, whose major contribution was to opera. Incidentally, 100 slides are enough to show in an hour.

If you know your subject and have something to offer an audience, charge a fee for your lectures and you will be well on your way back abroad. However tempting it might be to give in to a friend who asks you to speak gratis to her service club, insist on a fee. You have only to give one good lecture and you are well on your way. One club member probably has friends in another club, which also needs programs.

Another enterprising American, on his way to Europe, contacted people in his city (through advertisements, through friends, and through an international organization) who had relatives in Europe and promised to take pictures of them to bring back to the American branch of the family. He sold these pictures and prints, which the Americans were delighted to have, and paid most of his travel expenses doing it.

If selling is your field, you might get a commission as a sales representative from small local concerns. One American from Chicago did this and now has established an office abroad. He is now an American from Frankfurt.

Do you ski well? Ski enthusiasts in this country are all familiar with visiting ski instructors; many are unaware that the exchange works both ways. You might get a job as a ski instructor on the slopes in Switzerland or Italy.

A home economist from Wisconsin was unable to sell that state's governor on the idea of her personally escorting 500 pounds of Wisconsin cheese to servicemen in Korea, so she paid her own way and taught English to Japanese students when she got there. Her idea was turned down, incidentally, only because the cheese would have had to be shipped by air at a prohibitive cost.

This is just to help you start your thinking. You may find you have just the gimmick—and skills—to get a really different job abroad.

CHAPTER XIV

What Are the Chances of Becoming a Company Executive Abroad?

If you would be a good company executive at the home office, chances are fair that you would be a good company executive abroad. But don't expect to walk into the office of the international division personnel director and be handed an overseas assignment after a short training period. The road to an overseas appointment can be long and hard, but it can be yours if you're willing to work for it.

First, you must be willing to spend, at the very minimum, two years learning the company operation. An overseas executive must first be a "company man." He must know the company operation and policy in all its phases. He must be able to work well with company people. He must be convinced of the worth of the company's product or services and able to convey his confidence. He must have patience and energy as well as ideas.

Toward the end of your two- to five-year stint in the home office, your company will begin to send you out on assignments all over the country. If you perform well in these assignments, you might then be given your first test at an overseas task. This will normally be a short tour of four to six weeks, performing a specific job in a specific location. You may go as an assistant to an experienced overseas man or, on rare occasions, be sent alone. If your company makes large machinery, for example, your first assignment might be to sell, supervise installation, and teach the buyers how to use the product.

One international executive told of a man who had just returned from a similar test assignment in Iceland.

"He did his job well. No hitches. The equipment went right in. And he was well liked. Yes, he's due to go out again in three weeks."

After eight months to a year of short assignments, this young man will probably be on his way to more permanent assignments overseas. His performance is good, and this is of prime importance.

Running a close second, however, are factors that on the surface may not seem related to his job.

The candidate must be in good physical condition and able to withstand long working hours and difficult climates. If he drinks, he must be able to hold his liquor well and to control his drinking. This is estimated to be one of the major weaknesses of overseas executives, who often turn to liquor as an escape or out of sheer boredom.

He must be emotionally stable. If he is unable to cope with his problems at home, he certainly will not solve them by being transported to another country and placed in strange surroundings.

Equally important is his wife's stability. She must be totally devoted to her husband and to the job he is doing. She must be willing to trade her vacuum cleaner for a broom—possibly with a maid at the other end of it.

Of those overseas executives who don't make it—one estimate was higher than 50 per cent—the greatest single problem was the executive's wife. As one executive put it: "Nothing can make overseas personnel go to pot faster than an unhappy wife."

Despite investigations involving everyone from the company president to the staff psychologist, it is nearly impossible to tell beforehand how a wife will react overseas. The plumbing, her chief complaint, can and usually does go bad anywhere in the world. She must learn "kitchen Spanish" or "kitchen French" or whatever is spoken in the area to which she is sent. She must supervise the shopping, meal preparation, and housekeeping, as well as official entertaining.

One wife told of a luncheon invitation she had extended to a couple from India who were visiting the company's international office in Latin America. She had instructed her cook that this was to be a simple meal, since they were all to go out for a full dinner in the evening. What arrived, she said, was soup, salad, entree, vegetable, cheese, fruit, dessert, and finally, wine.

"We barely had time to stagger from this seven-course snack in time to dress for another seven courses in the evening. I really felt I didn't care if I never saw food again."

A wife's role of keeping the children content, the house clean, meals cooked, and shirts ironed cannot be more important anywhere —nor more difficult to accomplish—than it is overseas. Such minute details as purchasing a postage stamp or vegetables for the evening meal can be an all-day proposition in some parts of the world.

A company official in charge of international operations said that his company's first job was to keep the overseas families happy. And this included adequate schooling for the children. Schooling must be available, he felt, in nearby American or English schools, although some American families do send their children to local schools.

Executive positions abroad vary considerably from post to post. Here is a rundown of some of the posts to which United States businessmen are assigned, according to recent information published in *Business Week.*

London. Once you have acclimated yourself to the differences in language usage (a British woman "hoovers" her rugs, you arrive at your seventh floor office via a "lift," and you check your car's motor by lifting the "bonnet"), you will find business little different from home. It is conducted at a slower pace than in the United States, and you might find yourself working at the office until 7 P.M. A frequent request in a telephone conversation is: "Why don't you write me a letter?" Nearly 10,000 people comprise the American business community, which is the largest in Europe.

Paris. A business community of 7,000 to 8,000 people in Paris take their places quietly in French business. Since the French do not have large entertainment budgets, Americans do most of their entertaining at home, and then mostly for visiting American businessmen. Incidentally, entertaining visiting American "firemen" can be a chronic problem to American businessmen all over the world. Because in our country a businessman is generally expected to play an important role in the community, the American executive is frequently delighted at "just being left alone." This, however, may be the thing his wife misses in Paris—civic activities and the community atmosphere.

Milan. Connections are important and introductions almost mandatory in this rapidly expanding business community. Conversations lasting three to four hours are common and may tend toward philosophy and the fine arts, subjects dear to the hearts of many Italians. Selling capital goods to a few customers can involve delicate personal relationships, which many Americans feel incompetent to handle. Suburban living is almost unknown in Milan, and Americans tend to leave the city when they can for visits to Florence, Venice, Rome, and the Alpine lake resorts.

Zurich. Probably the best living in Western Europe is available in Zurich, but new Swiss regulations have worked a hardship on the

American businessman. Zurich is the headquarters for administration, sales, and technical services for many international companies because of its central location. Air service is easy and fast, and Americans say they see one another more at the airport than anywhere else in Zurich. Stores are well stocked, and a lakeside villa could be only a ten-minute drive from the office.

São Paulo. An American businessman stands out in São Paulo and is generally a real part of the "American colony." He is ignored by the Brazilian intellectuals and admired or envied by the businessmen. Usually political tension puts him in an unfavorable light. He is often strongly pro-Brazilian as well as pro-American and seems to try to maintain his life much as he would at home as a sort of protective covering. Americans working in São Paulo are very conscious of their "image" but confess that they enjoy working with Brazilians who tend to imitate American business methods.

Mexico City. The best executive talent American corporations can send is required in this top post. Mexico has a new class of shrewd businessmen, and the government regulations can be frustrating. Generally the Americans in Mexico City are happy to be there, and although they have formed a definite "American colony," more of them speak Spanish than anywhere else in Latin America. The barriers between the Mexicans and Americans are minimal. Businessmen generally work longer hours in Mexico City, but normally the pace is slower than in the United States.

Tokyo. Patience is a virtue that is required in Japan. If the American is unwilling to wait three hours on three consecutive days to see a Japanese executive, Tokyo is not the place for him. In the Oriental ritual of conducting business, the first meeting is simply social amenities, and the second might include tea. Then there is the visit to the "geisha" house, followed perhaps by an evening of nightclubs. Then, and only then, will business be conducted. The cost of living in Tokyo is very high. A house with central heating at $750 a month is a bargain. You must have a driver—to keep from getting lost—and most food is imported. American businessmen tend to know one another well because they frequently need the company of their own kind. Adaptation in Japan, while usually adequate for business purposes, is never quite complete.

One more point: Language facility is generally less necessary for the executive abroad than for an American on the lower echelons.

Usually an executive will have a native counterpart who will interpret for him.

While an executive may be bilingual—he may speak French, for example—the nature of his job often takes him to many parts of the world in the course of his business career where French or whatever language he has is not spoken.

In Japan, for example, there is a by-word among American businessmen that "if he speaks English, he doesn't make decisions." The Japanese "decision maker," even if he does speak English, will seldom confess to it.

Nine Tips to Remember When Traveling Abroad on Business

1. Be prepared for the language barrier. Your "in flight" time might be well spent studying a phrase book. If you have literature to leave with your contacts, have it printed in the local language, and list prices in the local currency instead of American dollars.

2. Have patience with overseas business attitudes as well as with late appointments. In some countries being on time is simply not done. On the other hand, in most of Europe—except Spain and Portugal—and in Australia and Hong Kong, being on time for appointments is most necessary.

3. Dress properly for an appointment with a foreign government or business official. Even in the tropics you should wear a suit when calling on a government official, even if he is in shirt sleeves. You may remove your coat, but only at his invitation. Generally it is well to wear a white shirt, but in France a colored or striped shirt is permitted.

4. Be aware of foreign social customs in your business dealings. Most Europeans are very reluctant to discuss personal affairs. If you meet a European businessman socially, never begin the conversation by asking what his job is, what his golf score is, or how many children he has. Conversely, an Indian will show he is interested in you by asking similar questions of you.

If you are invited to dinner in a home, you may take flowers to your hostess. In Europe take just a few, and never take chrysanthemums, since they are associated with funerals. In the Middle East, the dinner will be a strictly stag affair, and it would be improper for you even to ask about the host's wife or daughters. Never offer a Middle East businessman alcohol, which Muslims do not drink. At a Chinese dinner, you will take the seat facing the door, which is rigid social protocol.

In Europe you shake hands with a businessman when you leave as well as when you meet him, even if you meet him several times in the same day. A German businessman will help you with your coat when you are leaving and if he is also leaving, you will help him with his.

In a conference with many European businessmen, you begin by shaking hands with the senior officer and work your way down.

5. Small talk is important. It would be well to inform yourself of the newest developments in your host country and, if you can, show some knowledge of its history and culture as well as its national heroes. You may be amazed at how much your host knows about your country. Do him the courtesy of familiarizing yourself with his.

6. When making business calls, always telephone first. The best hours for a business appointment are between 10 and 11 A.M. and 3 and 4 P.M. The man who makes decisions may not even be in the office before 10 A.M. and if he is, he is probably dealing with the morning mail. After 4 P.M., he may be signing outgoing mail and before 3 P.M., you cannot be sure he will be back from lunch. In all Muslim countries, business is conducted Saturday through Thursday, with Friday off for the Muslim holy day. Saturday is the Sabbath in Israel, and in the Christian countries no business is conducted on Sunday. It is usually not wise to plan on much business being conducted on the day before the holy day, since this is usually the time for conferences and planning the next week's business.

7. Be prepared for the incidental costs of travel. Many foreign exchange companies and some United States banks provide tip-kits, pre-packaged foreign currency envelopes. If you don't have one of these, travel with 10 to 15 one dollar bills and about 20 quarters to take care of tips.

Your daily travel expenses in some of the major countries and areas in the world are roughly the following (exclusive of air fare).

Africa	$35–$45
Australia	$30–$35
Caribbean	$30–$35
Central America	$25–$30

Far East	$25–$35
France	$40–$50
Mexico	$30–$35
Middle East	$25–$35
Scandinavia	$25–$35
South America	$30–$35
Venezuela	$40–$50
Western Europe	$30

8. Be careful in your packing. In addition to the suggested lists given in Chapter XVI, here are some items you might include if you are a business executive abroad.

Take plenty of *business cards* (perhaps in two languages).

If you are taking a camera, be sure to take *film,* unless you are sure it is available where you are going.

Take several *small notebooks* or a supply of 3 x 5 cards to keep your records straight and portable.

Good *ballpoint pens* with plenty of *refills* are helpful.

Extra *passport photographs*—at least a dozen—may be needed in the Middle East or Africa.

If you wear *glasses,* take an extra pair as well as your prescription. Sunglasses are vital in many parts of the world.

Take plenty of your own *business letterheads* and contract forms. Hotel stationery is fine for tourists, but not for conducting business.

9. Plan your first days in a new city or country carefully. It is always well to arrive in a new area on the weekend to give yourself time to become acclimated to strange surroundings. Don't try to make a lot of business calls the first day to impress the home office. Buy a map and plan your calls. If you are staying in a hotel, ask the clerk to get you a driver who speaks English unless you are fluent in the language. The hotel telephone operator can also help you make your appointments, and she will appreciate a small tip for her services.

If you plan to call the home office, you may have to make a reservation for your call in advance.

In most countries, especially in Europe, temporary secretarial help is available. You might try the local office of Manpower Inc., which has offices in most of the major cities of Europe and in many other countries, too. If there is no local office of Manpower Inc., you might ask the hotel clerk about English-speaking secretarial help. As a last resort, you might be able to enlist the help of the secretary to one of your business associates, but this is usually not a good idea.

Always ask for business cards. They are not always available, but they will help you keep your records straight.

If you are in a hotel, treat the chief clerk or concierge well. He can be invaluable as a source of business information as well as an authority on foreign social customs. And he can help you find an interpreter if one is required.

CHAPTER XV

Work-Study Programs for Students Abroad

Ask any student and he'll tell you there is much more to learning than textbooks and lectures.

And for a student to broaden his education immeasurably, he often looks to study overseas.

Study abroad will enable you to become more intimately acquainted with people and how they live.

Assuming you are a student, whether at the graduate or undergraduate level, you can go abroad to study under one of many plans, although few of them will pay all of your expenses. Some programs, set up as scholarships and grants, will provide you with many of your expenses, others ask that you pay for your own transportation. Most of the all-expense plans are aimed at postgraduate study or lecturing in a foreign university.

Many university programs for undergraduates abroad are sponsored by American colleges and universities and provide the student with credits toward his degree.

Since the level and method of teaching at universities abroad are quite different from those in the United States, it is generally not advisable for you to enter a foreign university directly for study.

There is, for example, very little "campus life" as we know it in this country. Most students at foreign universities are older and more serious than their American counterparts. They attend lectures, study, occasionally engage in games of chess, study, read extensively, study, and go home. There are no weekly quizzes, compulsory attendance, or "assigned reading." Students rarely, if ever, engage in horseplay between classes. They may sit next to one another in class for a whole year and never speak. Informal meetings between students and faculty are rare, and a professor's inviting some of his students in for a "talk session" with coffee is unheard of.

Then, of course, language is a problem. Imagine yourself excitedly entering your first lecture at a foreign university. You arrive early, find yourself a seat, uncap your pen and open your notebook, and wait expectantly. The professor arrives, the lecture begins, and there you are, wishing you had practiced the language more. Suddenly all the idiomatic phrases you learned are gone and are supplanted by the technical language of a specialized field. The class is over and your notebook is blank.

Of course, this situation will not last long. As you become acclimated to the language, you will find yourself thinking in it. And eventually you will not bother to take notes in English—even mental translating takes too long.

Away from the classroom your life will be centered around other students, and the success of your study abroad will be determined by how well you are accepted by them, and this acceptance will depend largely on your own ability to make friends.

The programs sponsored by American schools are often the best way to study overseas. One of the most common is the "Junior Year Abroad" program. Such groups are usually accompanied by American faculty members, who ease them over the rough spots, and it can be a most exciting and meaningful experience. If you are a student interested in a program like this, check with your adviser or with your campus representatives.

The expense is considerable—travel, tuition, lodging, etc.—but financial help is often available.

It is possible to work to help defray some of the expense. It should be noted, though, that the pay for students is generally low and the hours are long. Work permit regulations as outlined in Chapter IV apply, and unskilled workers may find themselves in jobs that can be described only as menial.

If you would like to work while studying abroad, one of the first places you might check with is:

American Student Information Service
Jahnstrasse 56a
Frankfurt-am-Main, Germany

This group was founded in 1958 to find jobs for students. Under its system, you would fly to Europe on an ASIS-chartered plane and take part in a special tour before beginning work. The jobs include farm work, hotel, resort and camp posts, construction jobs, and hospital work. You would work from four to eight weeks and earn about $50 a month plus room and board, or $100 a month if you provide your own food and lodging.

The ASIS warns applicants:

"The European working day is probably longer and harder than you are accustomed to. You will have to adapt yourself to an entirely new environment. If you do not think you will be able to adapt, or if you are unprepared to work hard, you should not apply for a job."

Furthermore, your job may not even offer you an opportunity to meet the people and practice your language skills. It may be, as was one student's experience, that you would spend long hours washing dishes in a restaurant alone in a windowless room and after work be too tired to do anything but fall into bed.

This is, of course, not true of all work provided by the ASIS, but you must be prepared for it. Most employers will treat you well and take a real interest in your desire to learn the language and see the country. But it is well to know exactly what is expected of you on your job abroad.

There are other sources of work for you if you go abroad unskilled. We have already spoken about the *au-pair* arrangement for girls studying in France who live with a French family, do some housework, care for the children, and teach them English in return for room and board. Here is the address again for such family work placements in France:

L'Accueil Familial de Jeunes Étrangers
23 Rue de Cherche-Midi
Paris VI, France

Many student jobs are available in Germany for the summer months in agriculture, industry, hotels and restaurants, construction, child care, and such facilities as hospitals, sanitariums, and homes for the aged.

Students working in agriculture would help in the fields, tend livestock, and assist in house and garden work. They might also work for provincial departments on highway landscaping and forestry service.

In industry, opportunities occur on light machinery requiring no special skills, in the assembly of small parts, as inspectors of finished products, in loading and unloading goods, and as drivers' helpers on delivery trucks.

Hotel and restaurant work is available to students in Germany, including work in the kitchen and food service and as chambermaids and doormen.

Medical students with the requisite knowledge of German may be qualified to work as assistants in health facilities.

Girls who are able to work at least three months in Germany can get part-time jobs with families in housework and child care. Men can work in construction jobs, excavation and salvage work, concrete mixing, and other jobs related to the construction and repair of buildings and roads.

Wages generally range between 50 and 70 cents an hour, which is low by American standards but is considered adequate in Germany. You must be at least eighteen years of age, have a working knowledge of German, and be in a position to work for at least two months.

This program is offered by Lufthansa Airlines; you may get further information from its nearest office.

For other job information for Germany, write:

Zentralstelle für Arbeitsmittlung
Escherschemier Landstrasse 1–7
Frankfurt-am-Main, Germany

If you would like to work in Finland and do not speak Finnish, you might qualify for a traineeship in architecture, engineering, or the technical fields. For any other field, it is usually necessary to speak either Finnish or Swedish. The trainee programs function under the Ministry of Communications and Public Works and usually last from six to eighteen months.

An arrangement for living with a Finnish family, similar to the *au-pair* arrangement in France, is also available. Under such an arrangement, you would be expected to teach English to the family, possibly baby-sit and do light housework with other members of the family.

Male trainees may work on farms and would receive the standard salary of a Finnish farm worker.

If you would like to work in Finland, write a letter giving full details of your age, education, knowledge of languages, the field in which you would like a traineeship, and the length of your desired stay to:

Foreign Trainee Exchange Program
Mikonkatu 8 IX Floor
Helsinki, Finland

You can get information about agricultural and horticultural work in England by writing:

The Allied Circle
International Exchange Visits Department
46 Green Street, Park Lane
London, W. 1

or

Concordia (Youth Service Volunteers)
188 Brompton Road
London, S.W. 3

If you are a student in the general fields of commerce and economics and would like an opportunity for on-the-job training in another country, you might qualify for the exchange program sponsored by the Association Internationale des Étudiants en Sciences Économiques et Commerciales (AIESEC).

This program arranges for two- to six-month training assignments with foreign business firms in any of 24 member countries in Europe, North America, the Middle East, or Asia. Almost 200 universities are currently involved in the program. Applicants are expected to help the student committee on campus to find American companies that will take two foreign students under similar traineeships. They must expect to pursue a career in business and economics and should be upperclassmen or graduate students.

Under such a program you pay for your own transportation, but the firm for which you work provides a living allowance, which is usually about $70 a week for foreign students in this country. You might expect an allowance of between $60 to $80 a week, depending on the cost of living in the country in which you work.

If you are not certain whom to contact on your campus, you can get more information by writing:

Association Internationale des Étudiants en Sciences Économiques et Commerciales
51 East 42nd Street
New York, N.Y. 10017

A similar program for traineeships in science or engineering in industrial companies is also available. For information write:

International Association for the Exchange of Students for Technical Experience
345 East 47th Street
New York, N.Y. 10017

A summer work program is available in Israel for senior students of medicine, biology, architecture, chemistry, and engineering. Write:

The Professional and Technical Workers Aliyah
515 Park Avenue
New York, N.Y. 10022

Many other summer traineeship programs are available in other countries. If you are now in a college or university, check with the student placement bureau or with the departmental office in your major field. You might also get information from a country's embassy in this country (see Appendix C).

For a leaflet entitled "Educational Exchange Grants," containing complete information on many of the available grants, write:

Superintendent of Documents
U.S. Government Printing Office
Washington, D.C.

The Fulbright scholar is one of the best-known members of a scholastic exchange program. Since this program pays for all major expenses, it is usually not necessary for the student to take on outside work. The Fulbright program covers travel and living expenses, and if the student is under one of the special teaching or research grants, it may be possible for him to take his dependents.

You can get information on scholarships, grants, and all college-sponsored programs abroad from:

Counseling Division, Dept. V.M.
Institute of International Education
809 United Nations Plaza
New York, N.Y. 10017

This institute has prepared reports on university study in Europe, Asia, Africa, the Middle East, and Latin America and has a reference library of foreign university catalogs.

You as a student can get experience working abroad under volunteer service. Some of these programs pay part of the cost of your travel; others ask you to assume the full cost. Usually you pay for your own transportation and the service projects and work camps provide lodging and food.

Why might you want to go overseas under these conditions? The American Friends Service Committee, which sponsors overseas work camps, says:

"Work is universal. People of all countries and races must work, and tired muscles mean the same in any language. It is through doing constructive work, rather than merely reading or talking about human problems, that people come to understand the tensions and prejudices that separate individuals and nations."

You would live in simple surroundings and work at unskilled and often strenuous jobs. You might scrub floors, build a dormitory, repair a road, care for children in an orphanage, or help with a recreation program in a slum area.

You would meet young people from all over the world and have a real opportunity to know what living abroad can mean in terms of honest satisfaction. When not working, you would attend lectures and social events, take short trips, and meet people.

A complete list of work camps and service opportunities, as well as valuable information for students, is contained in a booklet entitled "Work, Study, Travel Abroad," published by the United States National Student Association. The booklet, which costs a dollar, is available by writing to the U.S.N.S.A., Educational Travel, Inc.:

265 Madison Avenue
New York, N.Y. 10016

or

1355 Westwood Boulevard
Los Angeles, California 90024

At the end of the section on work programs for students, the National Student Association warns:

"Job seekers are cautioned against signing contracts before careful investigation. Most employment agencies specializing in overseas employment are reputable agencies, but there are a few dishonest groups who advertise in newspapers and periodicals, offering employment overseas. The applicant often pays a fee for the agency's services and upon arrival abroad finds that he has been the victim of a swindle.

"Each year thousands of recent college graduates set off to Europe, with hopes of securing an exciting 'different' sort of job. After a brief sightseeing tour, many of these young people are forced to return home, for there are too few jobs available abroad for the multitude of American work-seekers."

CHAPTER XVI

Getting Ready for Your Trip

Get Ready. Get Set. Go! You have your job or are fairly certain you can get one overseas, and travel brochures are all over the floor. You are debating whether to go by ship or plane and which line is best for you. You are deeply involved in language study, and tomorrow you are going out to buy a new suitcase or two. You are checking newspaper ads to find easy-care clothing suitable for the climate you will be in for the next two months or the next two years. You have talked with friends who have been on a trip to where you are going, and your future working overseas looks bright.

Get Ready! How can you find out more about where you will be? Travel brochures are helpful, of course, but are often inclined to paint a rosy picture that may be slightly overdrawn. After all, you will not be spending long, lazy afternoons lolling on a beach. You may be pushing away a lank strand of hair as you work over a typewriter in a hot, humid climate—or shivering in a poorly heated room while what seems interminable rain pours down the window.

Of course, one of the best ways to plan for your trip abroad is to read everything you can find pertaining to the country of your choice. Your librarian can be of great help here. Take her advice and read, read, read, until either her supply is exhausted (try another library) or you are ready to pick up your suitcase and leave on your big adventure.

Studying the country will also be part of your language study, since the two go hand in hand. Keep your ears open for anything that might be helpful to you.

The foreign embassies in this country can be very helpful. Write to them outlining your plans briefly, and they will doubtless send reams of material and perhaps even forward your letter to the government tourist office—which will deluge you with more. Read it and make notes if that helps—but do it before you leave. You will be far too busy when you have arrived at your destination to find out about local currency and what toilet articles are readily available in the stores.

If you don't have much time to spend in intensive study, don't panic. In even a few weeks you can do some boning up that will help. You can start with a good encyclopedia, which will give you an intensive course in the most important historical and geographical facts about a country and also the currency exchange rates. Currency is one of the most difficult—and immediate—problems that an American faces abroad, and it is important—no, vital—that you master it.

Get a good map and study it until you can nearly draw it from memory, placing the major cities, rivers, and mountains. Learn the names and locations of areas as well—the high plains of the Andes, Andalucía in Spain, or the Jezreel plain in Israel. If you can get a detailed map of the city or area in which you will be working, so much the better.

Granted, all this study beforehand may tend to take the glamor and romance out of your dreams, but it will help you adjust much more readily to your new surroundings, not to mention giving you many happy hours planning for your trip.

While you are "getting ready" it is understood that you will learn as much about your future job as possible. Read and *understand* the terms of your contract—before you sign it. Know just what will be expected of you, and learn as much about the company as possible. Whether your work is the purpose for your trip or a means to an end, you will be expected to earn your salary. Your employer has a right to the best you can give him—so learn your job.

One final note should be added. While you are learning about the country, don't overlook the political climate, which can be vital to you overseas. The best place to learn about national politics is from a newspaper that reports foreign news in detail. In the East the New York *Times* is a good source. Check for any details, however small, that might be helpful. You will avoid thus the consternation one American faced in Greece when he ordered "Turkish coffee" the day after the Turks had bombed Cyprus, which the Greeks feel is their island. His waiter's facial muscles didn't relax the forced smile, but his eyes hardened.

Get Set! As the time approaches for your departure, you will apply for your passport, either at the passport office in the Post Office in the nearest big city, or at the Passport Division of the Department of State, Washington, D.C.

When applying for a passport, you must be able to prove your American citizenship by birth or baptismal certificate. In lieu of this, you may present an affidavit signed by your parents or someone else who has personal knowledge of the date and place of your birth. A previous passport can also be proof of citizenship. If you are a naturalized citizen, you must submit evidence of citizenship of the person through whom your claim is made.

Your application must include two recent photographs, one of which you will sign. The photos, which must be 2½ to 3 inches square, can be made by any photographer for a nominal fee. If you are to be accompanied by dependents, you must submit a group photograph.

In addition to proof of citizenship and photograph, you must also be able to establish your identity to the satisfaction of the passport agents or the court clerk. The following documents are acceptable for identification purposes provided they contain the signature and either a photograph or a physical description: a previous passport, a naturalization certificate, a driver's license, or a government, industrial, or business identification card or pass. An identifying witness (someone who has known you for at least two years) is required only when you cannot establish your identity any other way.

Passport fees are $10—$1 for processing the application and $9 for the passport. The latter must be in currency or postal money order payable to the Secretary of State.

In addition to passport application—and for some countries, visa applications—your work, residence, or immigration permits must be in order. Check with the consulate for information about what papers you must have.

Most countries require inoculations of some kind, and, unless you don't mind traveling with a sore arm, it is well to have them done as early as possible. Usually the health certificate is required only upon re-entry into the United States, but some foreign governments require it. Most inoculation records are valid for three years, so even if you have signed a contract for two years, get your shots before you leave home.

When your papers are in order, the next item of business is to pack your bags. If you are traveling by plane, you will be permitted to take 44 pounds of luggage on a tourist-class flight and 66 pounds in first class. Since the allowances include the weight of the luggage, and since you must pay extra for any excess weight, it is well to buy lightweight luggage. Make sure that the latches are strong. But no matter how confident you are, include a good strong strap, available at Army surplus stores, as one of the first items you pack.

If you are flying, plan to carry in your flight bag any items packed in pressurized cans or plastic squeeze bottles. These react in strange and inconvenient ways when tidily stowed away in your suitcase. By carrying them with you, you will avoid opening a suitcase to find shaving lotion or hair spray all over your new clothes.

The choice of items you should take with you depends on how long you are going to be abroad and where. Packing for one of the major cities of Europe and for the interior of Africa are very different matters.

Here, however, are some suggestions that might be helpful, and you can add or subtract items to fit your circumstances. But don't add too many. "Travel light" is the admonition of nearly everyone who has gone abroad. If in doubt as to whether to take something along, don't.

Nearly all of these items will fit into one suitcase; if they don't, take out what for you are the nonessentials.

For Men:

1 dark woolen suit
1 pair woolen slacks
2 wash-and-wear light suits
1 pair walking shoes
1 pair loafers
1 pair tennis shoes
1 pair bedroom slippers
2 sweaters
1 cotton bathrobe
1 raincoat or all-weather coat
1 pair foldup rubbers
1 cap, hat or rainhat
2 wash-and-wear cotton shirts
3 undershorts
2 pair wool socks
2 pair cotton socks

For Women:

1 knit suit
1 wool town suit
2 dressy blouses
2 casual blouses
2 sweaters
1 casual dress
1 afternoon dress
1 cocktail dress (basic black with jacket)
4 sets lingerie
2 pair cotton socks
6 pair hose (all the same color)
1 all-weather coat
2 nighties or pajamas
1 foldup robe and slippers
1 packable hat

For Men:

1 pair swimming trunks
3 summer polo shirts
1 scarf
6 ties
6 handkerchiefs
1 belt
1 pair sunglasses
1 bottle of aspirin
1 small tin of Band-Aids
1 bottle antiseptic
Shaving kit
Dressing case
Necessary medicines

For Women:

2 scarves
1 pair sandals
1 pair tennis shoes
1 pair walking shoes
1 pair black heels
1 bathing suit and cap
1 pair sunglasses
2 pairs gloves (short white and long
    black)
1 bottle of aspirin
Jewelry
1 small tin Band-Aids
Toilet articles
Rainboots
Perfume—sealed with wax
Necessary medicines

Needless to say, for warm climates this list could be reduced considerably. If you are going to take a camera, check first whether film is available at your destination or whether you should take it with you. You might want to include a few books, but take good ones—paperback, if possible.

You might want to include a World Almanac and a good history of the United States. William Miller's *History of the United States* (Dell) or the *Pocket History of the United States* by Allan Nevins and Henry Steele Commager (Pocket Books) are excellent. You might also like to include the newest edition of *Paperbound Books in Print* (Bowker), which might give your foreign friends an idea of the extent of cultural interests in America, and a few United States maps.

Some of these items will go into your flight bag if you are going by air. If your flight is to be a long one, include comfortable slippers or shoes in addition to toilet articles.

If you are going to a tropical climate, by all means get a copy of "Health Hints for the Tropics," published by the American Society of Tropical Medicine and Hygiene. This little booklet begins:

"It is well for travelers to the tropics to be neither too romantic nor too cynical about their destination. Those who consider the tropics a glamorous place where people live in exotic surroundings are likely to be lulled into a careless state of mind in which they do not give sufficient thought to health hazards. On the other hand, pessimists who refer to Africa as 'the white man's grave' go much too far in the other direction. They think only of danger, disease, and bad climate. Both of these extreme groups have the wrong attitude, and both have been misinformed. The truth, as usual, lies in between. The right attitude is the commonsense one, which seeks out the facts and then makes the proper adjustment to these facts.

"Let it be emphasized right at the start that life can be safe, comfortable, and pleasant under most tropical conditions. Tropical diseases in general are well understood, are preventable, are for the most part susceptible to cure by modern methods, and are not the mysterious maladies or unknown fevers so often referred to in popular fiction."

The booklet, which outlines in detail information about immunizations, medicines, and general health precautions, can be obtained by sending 50 cents to:

Editor
Tropical Medicine and Hygiene News
Bethesda, Maryland

Go! There are some things that you should most certainly take with you and that will not add an ounce to your already overstuffed suitcase. These are the things that make up your mental luggage.

One of the most important is your attitude toward your own country. You will arrive on foreign soil with the unique label "American," and you must be prepared for it. You may be the only American your new friends have seen up close, and their questions will be as varied as they are unexpected.

While you are boning up on the country to which you are going, make sure you are familiar with the United States and its method of government. Be able to explain the difference between Congress and the state legislatures. Know the names of our leading politicians, including the present Cabinet members, and of some of the living Americans who have made significant contributions to world culture.

Be prepared for questions about civil rights and integration, juvenile delinquency, foreign policy, the divorce rate, and Indian reservations.

You can risk trying to bluff your way through some of these questions, which will lead you deeper and deeper into the mire of your own lack of understanding, or you can lamely concede these points. Or you can argue, loudly and vehemently, which will serve no useful purpose except to give your questioners more ammunition.

Dr. Paul R. Conroy, Chief of Professional Training at the United States Information Agency, has some valuable suggestions for Americans drawn into such discussions.

The first rule is, don't argue. No one wins an argument, which usually disintegrates in two people shouting at one another, neither listening to what the other has to say.

Second, answer with a "Yes, but have you considered . . ." technique. This, of course, means that you must hear him out, but it will show him that you are willing to listen.

Third, find out what the critic has in mind, what is really bothering him. If he says "Americans have no culture," explain that culture is a word with a lot of meanings. If he says that most of our music seems to be rock and roll, and when Beethoven is heard, however rarely, it is interrupted every five minutes for a commercial. You then have at least found a subject of conversation—music in America—and the facts to give your critic.

Fourth, draw on your own experience. Get the discussion down to personal experiences. In criticism of radio commercials, you might agree that some of them are indeed irritating, but that you have also heard complete operas broadcast from the Metropolitan, with commercials only between acts and at the end, or that there is a small amateur symphony in your town. After all, people have their own ways of trying to provide opportunities to enjoy the better things in life, and our way seems to have worked out pretty well for us.

Fifth, get the discussion out of an exclusively American context. Problems of prejudice and discrimination are universal. Try to avoid making a situation-by-situation comparison of his country and yours, but keep the discussion as general as possible, at least until you find out whether your questioner wants honest answers or is trying to needle you.

Sixth and last, be reasonable. Your manner will be remembered much longer than what you say, and if you give courteous consideration to your critic, you will have made a good impression on him and anyone listening to the conversation. Be frank. If you don't know the answer to his question, admit it. Say you will try to find out, and arrange a time when you will have the information for him. If he becomes argumentative, you might point out that there are many people in the United States who agree with him, but that there are also other opinions. You might even admit that whatever situation he is criticizing does pose a problem for the United States and ask if he has any suggestions. People are flattered by being asked their opinions.

Dr. Conroy concludes: "Remember that you are not always going to convince everyone in one sitting, but you will have gone far if you leave the impression that there is something in the U.S. point of view."

The American Council for Nationalities Service has published an excellent booklet entitled "Americans Abroad—Questions You'll Be Asked About Your Country." In addition to general information about the "do's and don'ts" of international conversation, it gives specific suggestions for answers to questions in the general fields of peace and disarmament, the cold war, economic aid, military aid, and American life and attitudes.

Here, from the booklet, is a typical question and its answer:

"Why do you have so much crime and violence in America?"

"Emphasis on crime and violence in the press and in our films and television may be misleading. Americans are probably neither more or less law-abiding than other peoples.

"Crime and violence, unfortunately, make news; peace and quiet do not. So, when violence breaks out in one city as its white and Negro children begin attending school together, it is news at home and around the world. It is not news when another city integrates its schools without violence.

"We Americans traditionally focus attention on evil and injustice so that they can be dealt with, and strongly disapprove of sweeping the seamy side of life under the rug. We feel that public exposure of evil, embarrassing though it might be, is far better than hiding it.

"Admittedly, there is more crime and violence in the United States than we wish to see. But they exist everywhere in the world—and from much the same causes. We think we are making progress in removing some of the causes, such as ignorance, slums, economic injustice, and racial discrimination."

This booklet, which makes good reading for any American, would be especially helpful for anyone going abroad. For your copy, send 25 cents to:

American Council for Nationalities Service
20 West 40th Street
New York, N.Y.

The second important bit of mental luggage to take with you is the understanding that people are people everywhere, regardless of the way they dress, their language, and their customs. Accepting them as you hope they will accept you will be the key to your success with your new friends.

"So You're Going to Represent Us (U.S.) Abroad!" a delightful booklet written for A.I.D. employees and illustrated with telling cartoons, is aimed at providing Americans with just this bit of mental luggage.

It discusses your attitude toward the local religion, the role of women, proper attire for conducting business, first-name familiarity, and food and drink. In the last category, which is an awkward subject at best, the booklet advises: "If you do take a social highball, determine your capacity and then divide it by two. This will prevent your leaving the party with the lampshade for a hat or disclosing the secret war plans of the associated powers."

The booklet concludes: "The matter of 'face' is a cardinal law of the areas where we are working. While 'face' is an intangible something, it might be sobering to remember that wars have been fought over 'face-saving' reasons. To avoid losing face, keep in mind a few rules.

(a) Do not talk down to your foreign friends; they're probably as well equipped as you are for their life and existence.

(b) Do not berate a host country national in public. To do so will create a lifelong enemy because you've been the cause of his losing face.

(c) Do not make fun of their methods, ability, and tools; they've built the Pyramids and the Great Wall of China without our help and with the funny methods you criticize.

(d) And finally, do not be a name dropper. Unless you actually are what you claim to be and have been the lifelong pal of the

King of Something or Other, the truth will eventually come out and there goes your 'face' permanently."

If you would like a copy of this booklet, write to:

Orientation and Counseling Branch
Career Development Division, A/PA
Department of State
Agency for International Development
Washington, D.C.

And last and probably the most important item is your sense of humor, which will bear you through all kinds of embarrassing and frustrating situations. If you don't take yourself so seriously that the slightest thing becomes a major offense, you will find that your stay abroad is in every sense an exciting, delightful experience.

Get ready. Get set. Go!

And bon voyage!

Department of Commerce Field Offices

Albuquerque, N.M. (87101)—U.S. Courthouse.

Anchorage, Alaska (99501)—Room 60, U.S. Post Office and Courthouse.

Atlanta, Ga. (30303)—4th Floor, Home Savings Building, 75 Forsyth Ave., N.W.

Birmingham, Ala. (35203)—Title Building, 2028 Third Avenue, N.

Boston, Mass. (02110)—Room 230, 80 Federal Street.

Buffalo, N.Y. (14203)—504 Federal Building, 117 Ellicott Street.

Charleston, S.C. (29401)—No. 4 North Atlantic Wharf.

Cheyenne, Wyoming (82001)—207 Majestic Building, 16th and Capitol Avenue.

Chicago, Ill. (60606)—Room 1302, 226 West Jackson Boulevard.

Cincinnati, Ohio (45202)—809 Fifth Third Bank Building, 36 East 4th Street.

Cleveland, Ohio (44101)—4th Floor, Federal Reserve Bank Building, East 6th Street and Superior Avenue.

Dallas, Tex. (75201)—Room 3-104 Merchandise Mart, 500 South Ervay Street.

Detroit, Michigan (48226)—438 Federal Building.

Greensboro, N.C. (27402)—Room 407, U.S. Post Office Building.

Hartford, Conn. (06103)—18 Asylum Street.

Honolulu, H.I. (96813)—202 International Savings Building, 1022 Bethel Street.

Houston, Tex. (77002)—5102 Federal Building, 515 Rusk Avenue.

Jacksonville, Fla. (32202)—512 Greenleaf Building, 204 Laura Street.

Kansas City, Mo. (64106)—Room 2011, 911 Walnut Street.

Los Angeles, Calif. (90015)—Room 450, Western Pacific Building, 1031 South Broadway.

Memphis, Tenn. (38103)—212 Falls Building, 22 North Front Street.

Miami, Fla. (33132)—408 Ainsley Building, 14 N.E. First Avenue.

Milwaukee, Wis. (53203)—1201 Straus Building, 238 West Wisconsin Avenue.

Minneapolis, Minn. (55401)—Room 304, Federal Building, 110 South 4th Street.

New Orleans, La. (70130)—1508 Masonic Temple Building, 333 Saint Charles Avenue.

New York, N.Y. (10001)—61st Floor, Empire State Building, 350 Fifth Avenue.

Philadelphia, Pa. (19107)—Jefferson Building, 1015 Chestnut Street.

Phoenix, Arizona (85025)—New Federal Building, 230 North 1st Street.

Pittsburgh, Pa. (15222)—1030 Park Building, 355 Fifth Avenue.

Portland, Ore. (97204)—217 Old U.S. Courthouse, 520 S.W. Morrison Street.

Reno, Nevada (89502)—1479 Wells Avenue.

Richmond, Va. (23240)—2105 Federal Building, 400 North 8th Street.

St. Louis, Mo. (63103)—2511 New Federal Building, 1520 Market Street.

Salt Lake City, Utah (84101)—222 S.W. Temple Street.

San Francisco, Calif. (94011)—Room 419 Customhouse, 555 Battery Street.

Santurce, Puerto Rico (00907)—605 Condado Avenue, Room 628.

Savannah, Ga. (31402)—235 U.S. Courthouse and Post Office, 125–29 Bull Street.

Seattle, Wash. (98104)—809 Federal Office Building, 909 First Avenue.

American Chambers of Commerce in Foreign Countries

ARGENTINA
 Chamber of Commerce of the U.S.A. in the Argentine Republic
 Avenida R.S. Pena 567
 Buenos Aires

AUSTRALIA
 American Chamber of Commerce in Australia
 11th Level, Kindserley House
 33 Bligh Street
 Sydney

BELGIUM
 American Chamber of Commerce in Belgium
 21 Rue du Commerce
 Brussels

BRAZIL–RIO DE JANEIRO
 American Chamber of Commerce for Brazil–Rio de Janeiro
 Avenido Rio Branco 90
 Rio de Janeiro

BRAZIL–SÃO PAULO
 American Chamber of Commerce for Brazil–São Paulo
 Rue Formosa 367
 São Paulo

CHILE
 Chamber of Commerce of the U.S.A. in the Republic of Chile
 Bandera 84
 Santiago

CHINA (TAIWAN)
American Chamber of Commerce of Taipei, Taiwan
Chung Shan Road, No. 2nd Sec., 3rd floor
#47 Taipei

DOMINICAN REPUBLIC
American Chamber of Commerce of the Dominican Republic
Post Office Box 343
Santo Domingo

ENGLAND
American Chamber of Commerce in London, Inc.
75 Brook Street
London, W.1

FRANCE
American Chamber of Commerce in France, Inc.
21 Avenue George V
Paris 8

GERMANY
American Chamber of Commerce in Germany
1 Berlin 12
4 Fasanenstrasse
Berlin

Hinter dem Schutting
P. O. Box 73
Bremen

12 Rossmarkt
Frankfurt/Main

1 Tesdorpfstrasse
Hamburg

26 Marienplatz
Munich

IRELAND
U.S. Chamber of Commerce in Ireland
27 Merrion Square
Dublin 2

ITALY
American Chamber of Commerce for Italy
12 Via Agnello
Milan

Via Valfonda 9
Florence

Via XX Settembre N. 31
Genoa

Piazza de Spagna No. 15
Rome

Via Massena 20
Turin

JAPAN
American Chamber of Commerce in Japan
701 Tosho Bldg.
14, 3 chome
Marunouchi, Chiyoda-ku, Tokyo

KOREA
American Chamber of Commerce in Korea
Bando Building, Room 214
Seoul

MEXICO
American Chamber of Commerce in Mexico
Lucerna 78, Esq. Viena
Mexico 6, D.F.

NETHERLANDS
American Chamber of Commerce in the Netherlands
Laan van Meerdervoort 55
The Hague

PHILIPPINES
American Chamber of Commerce of the Philippines, Inc.
Elks Club Building, Dewey Boulevard
Manila

OKINAWA
Chamber of Commerce of the U.S. in Okinawa
P. O. Box 58
Koza

SPAIN
American Chamber of Commerce in Spain
Ramblo Estudios 109
Barcelona 2

Disputacion 8
Bilbao

San Augustin 2
Madrid

Ave. Queipo de Llano 13
Seville

Munoz Degrain 2
Valencia

Coso 15
Zaragoza

THAILAND
American Chamber of Commerce in Thailand
103 Patpong Road
Bangkok

URUGUAY

Chamber of Commerce of the U.S.A. in Uruguay
Rincon 723
Montevideo

VENEZUELA

American Chamber of Commerce in Venezuela
Apartado del Este 51811
Caracas

Major Embassies in Washington, D.C.

AFGHANISTAN

Embassy of Afghanistan
2341 Wyoming Avenue, N.W.
20008

ALGERIA

Embassy of the Democratic and
    Popular Republic of Algeria
2200 R Street, N.W.
20008

ARGENTINA

Embassy of the Argentine Republic
1600 New Hampshire Avenue, N.W.
20009

AUSTRALIA

Embassy of Australia
1700 Massachusetts Avenue, N.W.
20036

AUSTRIA

Embassy of Austria
2343 Massachusetts Avenue, N.W.
20008

BELGIUM

Embassy of Belgium
3330 Garfield Street, N.W.
20008

BOLIVIA

Embassy of Bolivia
Suite B 1250,
3636 16th Street, N.W.
20010

BRAZIL

Brazilian Embassy
3007 Whitehaven Street, N.W.
20008

BULGARIA

Legation of the People's Republic
of Bulgaria
2100 16th Street, N.W.
20009

BURMA

Embassy of the Union of Burma
2300 S Street, N.W.
20008

BURUNDI

Embassy of the Kingdom of Burundi
2018 R Street, N.W.
20008

CAMEROON

Embassy of the Federal Republic of
    Cameroon
5420 Colorado Avenue, N.W.
20011

CANADA

Embassy of Canada
1746 Massachusetts Avenue, N.W.
20036

CENTRAL AFRICAN
    REPUBLIC

Embassy of the Central African Re-
    public
1618 22nd Street, N.W.
20008

CEYLON

Embassy of Ceylon
2148 Wyoming Avenue, N.W.
20008

CHAD

Embassy of the Republic of Chad
1132 New Hampshire Avenue, N.W.
20037

CHILE   Embassy of Chile
                               1736 Massachusetts Avenue, N.W.
                               20036

CHINA   Chinese Embassy
                               2311 Massachusetts Avenue, N.W.
                               20008

COLOMBIA   Embassy of Colombia
                               2118 Leroy Place, N.W.
                               20008

COSTA RICA   Embassy of Costa Rica
                               2112 S Street, N.W.
                               20008

CZECHOSLOVAKIA   Embassy of the Czechoslovak Social-
                                   ist Republic
                               2349 Massachusetts Avenue, N.W.
                               20008

DENMARK   Embassy of Denmark
                               3200 Whitehaven Street, N.W.
                               20008

DOMINICAN REPUBLIC   Embassy of the Dominican Republic
                               1715 22nd Street, N.W.
                               20008

FINLAND   Embassy of Finland
                               1900 24th Street, N.W.
                               20008

FRANCE   Embassy of the French Republic
                               2535 Belmont Road, N.W.
                               20008

GERMANY   Embassy of the Federal Republic
                                     of Germany
                                 4645 Reservoir Road, N.W.
                                 20007

GREAT BRITAIN   British Embassy
                                 3100 Massachusetts Avenue, N.W.
                                 20008

GREECE   Embassy of Greece
                                 2221 Massachusetts Avenue, N.W.
                                 20008

INDIA   Embassy of India
                                 2107 Massachusetts Avenue, N.W.
                                 20008

INDONESIA   Embassy of the Republic of Indo-
                                     nesia
                                 2020 Massachusetts Avenue, N.W.
                                 20036

IRAN   Embassy of Iran
                                 3005 Massachusetts Avenue, N.W.
                                 20008

IRELAND   Embassy of Ireland
                                 2234 Massachusetts Avenue, N.W.
                                 20008

ISRAEL   Embassy of Israel
                                 1621 22nd Street, N.W.
                                 20008

ITALY   Embassy of Italy
                                 1601 Fuller Street, N.W.
                                 20009

JAPAN

Embassy of Japan
2520 Massachusetts Avenue, N.W.
20008

JORDAN

Embassy of the Hashemite Kingdom
    of Jordan
2319 Wyoming Avenue, N.W.
20008

KOREA

Embassy of Korea
2320 Massachusetts Avenue, N.W.
20008

MEXICO

Embassy of Mexico
2829 16th Street, N.W.
20009

NETHERLANDS

Embassy of the Netherlands
4200 Linnean Avenue, N.W.
20008

NEW ZEALAND

Embassy of New Zealand
19 Observatory Circle, N.W.
20008

NIGERIA

Embassy of Nigeria
1333 16th Street, N.W.
20036

NORWAY

Embassy of Norway
3401 Massachusetts Avenue, N.W.
20007

PAKISTAN

Embassy of Pakistan
2315 Massachusetts Avenue, N.W.
20008

PANAMA

Embassy of Panama
2601 29th Street, N.W.
20008

PERU   Embassy of Peru
                              1320 16th Street, N.W.
                              20036

PHILIPPINES   Embassy of the Philippines
                              1617 Massachusetts Avenue, N.W.
                              20036

PORTUGAL   Embassy of Portugal
                              2125 Kalorama Road, N.W.
                              20008

RUMANIA   Embassy of the Rumanian People's
                                 Republic
                              1601 22nd Street, N.W.
                              20008

SAUDI ARABIA   Embassy of Saudi Arabia
                              2233 Wisconsin Avenue, N.W.
                              20008

SOUTH AFRICA   Embassy of South Africa
                              3051 Massachusetts Avenue, N.W.
                              20008

SPAIN   Embassy of Spain
                              2700 15th Street, N.W.
                              20009

SWEDEN   Embassy of Sweden
                              2249 R Street, N.W.
                              20008

SWITZERLAND   Embassy of Switzerland
                              2900 Cathedral Avenue, N.W.
                              20008

SYRIAN ARAB REPUBLIC   Embassy of the Syrian Arab Republic
2144 Wyoming Avenue, N.W.
20008

THAILAND   Embassy of Thailand
2300 Kalorama Road, N.W.
20008

TURKEY   Embassy of the Republic of Turkey
1606 23rd Street, N.W.
20008

UNITED ARAB REPUBLIC   Embassy of the United Arab Republic
2310 Decatur Place, N.W.
20008

URUGUAY   Embassy of Uruguay
2362 Massachusetts Avenue, N.W.
20008

VENEZUELA   Embassy of Venezuela
2445 Massachusetts Avenue, N.W.
20008

National Holidays

January 1	Cameroon, Haiti, Sudan	May 17	Norway
		May 25	Argentina
January 4	Burma	May 27	Afghanistan
January 11	Chad	May 31	South Africa
January 26	Australia, India		
		June 1	Tunisia
February 4	Ceylon	June 2	Italy
February 6	New Zealand	June 10	Portugal
February 16	Lithuania	June 11 (1965)	Great Britain
February 18	Nepal	June 12	Philippines
February 24	Estonia	June 17	Iceland
February 25	Kuwait	June 23	Luxembourg
February 27	Dominican Republic	June 30	Congo (Kinshasa)
March 3	Morocco		
March 11	Denmark	July 1	Burundi, Canada, Ghana Rwanda, Somalia
March 23	Pakistan		
March 25	Greece		
		July 5	Venezuela
April 4	Hungary, Senegal	July 6	Malawi
April 17	Syrian Arab Republic	July 14	France, Iraq
		July 18	Spain
April 26	Tanzania		
April 27	Sierra Leone, Togo		
April 29	Japan		
April 30	Netherlands	July 20	Colombia
		July 21	Belgium
May 6 (1965)	Israel	July 22	Poland
May 9	Czechoslovakia	July 23	Ethiopia, United Arab Republic
May 11	Laos		
May 14	Paraguay		

July 26	Liberia	October 1	Cyprus, Nigeria
July 28	Peru	October 2	Guinea
		October 9	Uganda
August 1	Dahomey, Switzerland	October 10	China
		October 14	Madagascar
August 2 (1965)	Jamaica (First Monday in August)	October 24	Zambia
		October 26	Iran
		October 29	Turkey
August 6	Bolivia	November 1	Algeria, Vietnam
August 7	Ivory Coast		
August 10	Ecuador	November 3	Panama
August 15	Congo (Brazzaville), Korea	November 7 & 8	Union of Soviet Socialist Republics
August 17	Gabon, Indonesia	November 11	Sweden
August 23	Rumania	November 12	Saudi Arabia
August 25	Uruguay	November 14	Jordan
August 31	Malaysia, Trinidad and Tobago	November 18	Latvia
		November 22	Lebanon
		November 28	Mauritania
September 7	Brazil	November 29	Yugoslavia
September 9	Bulgaria		
September 15	Costa Rica, El Salvador, Guatemala, Honduras, Nicaragua	December 1	Central African Republic
		December 5	Thailand
		December 6	Finland
		December 11	Upper Volta
September 16	Mexico	December 12	Kenya
September 18	Chile	December 18	Niger
September 22	Mali	December 24	Libya
September 26	Yemen		

Bibliography

In addition to the sources already mentioned, including the many excellent government publications, these reference works were most valuable:

Angel, Juvenal L., *Looking for Employment in Foreign Countries,* 5th edition, World Trade Academy Press, 1961.

Casewit, Curtis W., *How to Get a Job Overseas,* Arco, 1965.

Ford, Norman D., *How to Travel and Get Paid for It,* 8th edition, Harian Publications, 1963.

Garraty and Adams, *A Guide to Study Abroad,* Channel Press, 1962.

Temple, C. Robert, *Americans Abroad,* Bold Face Books, 1961.

United States National Student Association, *Work Study Travel Abroad,* 1964.

Walker, James F., *Foreign Jobs,* Vantage Press, 1964.

Winfield, Louise, *Living Overseas,* Public Affairs Press, 1962.

More ARCO Books for School and Career Guidance

THE STUDENT'S GUIDE
Sir John Adams

Knowing the right way to study is half the battle; and this book, written for high school and college students contains many suggestions, procedures and guidelines to help you master **any** subject. Included are study schedules, memory techniques, reading abilities, use of text and reference books, note taking, essay writing, preparing for examinations and more. "For the student with intellect and curiosity, this book has sparkling but sound suggestions on how to be not only a good student but a good person."—**Choice. ($1.45)**

HOW TO BECOME A SUCCESSFUL STUDENT
Otis D. Froe & Maurice A. Lee

A practical guide in methods of study and learning. This book will help you to learn how to read and listen effectively, take quizzes and tests, use educational resources and facilities, reach the top in scholastic efficiency, learn the most with a minimum of effort and time, take good notes and set up a study schedule. **($1.25)**

COLLEGIAN'S GUIDE TO PART-TIME EMPLOYMENT
Russell Granger

A factual guide for all those students who want to work part-time while going to college. Information about the jobs available, how much time they take, what they pay and how to apply for them. Suggestions for operating a small business of your own are also included. **(95c)**

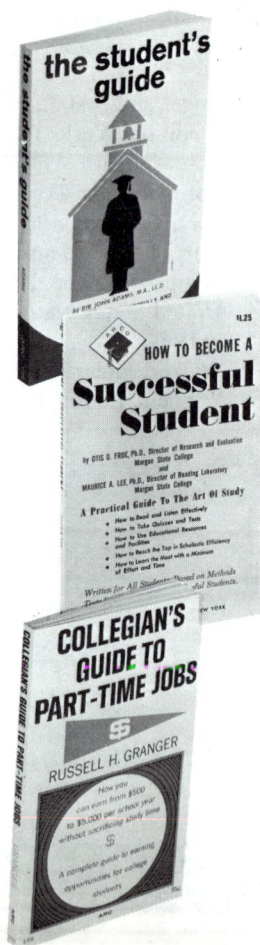